Library Construction
from a Staff Perspective

To the patrons of Williamsburg Regional Library, who voted to build a new facility, endorsed expansion of another, and displayed unremitting patience during the entire construction process. Without these citizens of Williamsburg, James City County and Upper York County, WRL would not be the excellent library system that it is today.

And to Patsy Hansel for her ten years as director of the Williamsburg Regional Library. Her vision and temerity contributed mightily to Williamsburg Regional Library's prominence in the community, and to the finished products at James City County Library and Williamsburg Library in particular. Thanks, Patsy. We'll miss you.

— The Library Staff

# Library Construction from a Staff Perspective

*by*

The Staff of the
Williamsburg Regional Library

McFarland & Company, Inc., Publishers
*Jefferson, North Carolina, and London*

Cover photographs: *(top)* groundbreaking; *(bottom)* interior of the Williamsburg Regional Library *(photograph by David Scherer)*.

ISBN 0-7864-0838-3 (softcover : 60# alkaline paper) ∞

Library of Congress cataloguing data are available

British Library cataloguing data are available

Manufactured in the United States of America

*McFarland & Company, Inc., Publishers*
*Box 611, Jefferson, North Carolina 28640*
*www.mcfarlandpub.com*

# Contents

# Introduction: From the Administrative Perspective

For much of the 1990s, the board and staff of the Williamsburg Regional Library (WRL) were involved in various stages of two building projects: new construction for a 35,000 square foot building that opened in 1996 (James City County Library — JCCL), and renovation and new construction that took a 28,000 square foot library to 40,000 square feet that opened in 1998, but for which the parking was not completed until 1999 (Williamsburg Library — WL).

In planning for these buildings, staff went through the steps that libraries generally go through in developing construction projects: determining the priorities for library services for the building, translating that into a building program, working with architects to make certain the building design meets the functional program needs, and cooperating with project managers and contractors to ensure that decisions arising after construction begins are made as quickly and effectively as possible. There are many texts that cover the basic steps in organizing a successful construction project, so we will not be concentrating on that in this book. Our purpose is to provide a perspective not so often found in the library literature on building libraries: the perspective of the staff who work in the library systems where the construction occurs.

Construction projects inspire a range of emotions in library employees, from the initial excitement to the postpartum depression that occurs when one realizes that the construction project is complete and (1) it is not perfect and (2) it does not solve all the library's problems, whether building related or not. However, most of those who worked at WRL during these two building projects are generally happy with the results, as are most of the patrons who talk to us about it. Our favorite patron comment about JCCL: "The building is a wedding of books and light, which gives wings to the spirit

1

as a library should." Our favorite patron comment about WL and the great service the staff provided throughout the construction and renovation at that library: "The ... 'E' flags." The library deserved an E for excellence, mimicking the World War II practice of awarding outstanding businesses bright "E" flags.

A brief history of the WRL is in order here. WRL's first public incarnation was an operation opened out of a private home in 1908 by Mary Haldane Begg Coleman and Anne Turner Chapman with 50 volumes from the Virginia State Library. It was not until 1973 that the public library gained a permanent location as the Williamsburg Library. WL served the growing community of the city of Williamsburg, James City County, and Upper York County, with the addition of an arts center theater and children's library wing in 1982.

The Williamsburg Regional Library is, as its name implies, a regional system with a governing board. We receive funding from three localities in addition to state funding, and our two projects fell under two different local governments.

By writing this book we hoped to explain how a good library building can be designed and constructed in a timely way with staff input, without antagonizing your municipal funders or the construction professionals. We wanted to share our experiences with the process, the people, and the materials, in order that other library staffs can learn from them.

We hope this volume will provide answers to questions you have and anticipate questions you will have. We wish you luck and success in your expansion or building project, and we're happy to have you contact us for further information or a visit.

As we edited this book, we realized that much of it sounds negative. Overall we were very pleased with the results from both building projects. However, what startled us at the time were the things that didn't go perfectly, so we thought most readers would be interested in hearing about those.

In the following chapters, library staff from different departments talk about what they saw as the most important tasks they worked on during the construction projects. They discuss areas where they think they did well and where they hope they can offer some advice to help others do better. We tried to come up with specific examples of what are pretty common issues in library construction, and how the WRL staff dealt with them.

A big thing to remember when trying to get staff involved in planning library construction projects is that new construction is easier than addition and renovation projects. When people have good ideas for a new building, those ideas can often be incorporated into the plans, with money usually setting the ultimate limit on what you can do. With an addition or renovation project, you're working around so much that cannot be changed (in our case, a central core of stacks that hold up the mezzanine — no point in suggesting that shelving would work better somewhere else) that there just are not as many options. For this reason we found that even though we tried to provide equivalent opportunities for staff involvement in both projects, many people felt that there was less opportunity for staff participation on the addition and renovation project.

I was director at WRL for ten years. It just so happened that at each of my earlier public library stops during my career, the libraries were involved in building projects. From that experience, I drew some conclusions that continued to hold true through the projects at WRL:

1. Architects, engineers, interior designers, and others of their ilk are wonderful, knowledgeable, creative people. However, they are committed to their professions first, and to your library needs second, just as we library people are first committed to library needs and only second to incidentals like aesthetics or how many columns are required to hold the roof up. So, hire the best people you can for all these jobs, and treat them as friendly adversaries; i.e., watch them like hawks. When in doubt, they will, with the best interest of your project in mind, defer to their own ideas, because those are the ones with which they are most comfortable. It is your responsibility to train them in library stuff. Even (maybe particularly) if they have lots of library experience, you must make it clear what is most important for your library staff to provide the best library service to your community. Sometimes, they will hear this most clearly if staff themselves do the talking.

2. No matter how hard you try to cover all the details, you will miss some things. In the long run, however, everything will work out fine.

3. During the process, you will agonize over certain decisions (whether to have moveable or permanent stanchions for your queuing lines, for example). You will decide on something revolutionary (permanent stanchions), and fret for months over whether this will be a major disaster that will be the end of your career. A year later you will realize that the big risk has turned into part of the library's standard way of doing business and you will marvel that it seemed such a big deal at the time. On the other hand, though you gnash your teeth in frustration at all the wonderful ideas you offer that are not implemented, after the library opens you will completely forget what they were, since the way things were done worked out just fine.

4. You will say to yourself that your library is so busy that you cannot possibly take on a task as big as working on a construction project. You will do so anyway, and you will love learning new things every day, and you will glory in the results — even though they will not be perfect.

5. If you are wise, you will make sure your library contact on the construction project makes friends with the contractor, the subcontractors, and whoever else is in charge of the bricks and mortar. We know we need to communicate with the architects, et al., at the outset of the project, but we tend to forget those who make our cherished plans real. The more the library contact learns to talk their language, the more the library will benefit from what they have to offer, particularly their ideas about how to do things a little differently and save money, which can be applied toward all those extras you wanted but didn't think you could afford.

6. Perhaps the most important lesson to be learned — and it is best to have absorbed this lesson before you begin even considering library construction — is that you must keep your sense of humor. Things will go wrong, no matter how carefully you plan. When they do, try to see the funny side. If construction causes your air conditioning to go down during the hottest week of the summer, you can consider it a major problem or you can adapt to the situation by declaring it shorts and T-shirt week ("naked library week" is probably a little bit too much fun). A sense of humor will go a long way toward minimizing staff and patron stress levels that construction undoubtedly will raise. You can go crazy or you can laugh. We recommend the latter and have tried to follow our own advice as much as possible. Admittedly, it is easier to see the humor in things after the problems are solved.

7. Related to number 6 is one more rule: Don't forget to have fun. Working on construction projects is a learning experience for everybody involved, gives library people a chance to get to know construction people a little better, and generally widens our horizons. And what is more fun than getting to know lots of new people and learning lots of new things? Enjoy.

In closing, I would like to say that special acknowledgment must go to the Book Committee members for their tireless efforts to synthesize their thoughts, draft chapters, brainstorm about content, and fit meetings in between their regular work, in order to bring this book to fruition.

Patsy Hansel
Director of WRL, 1989–1999

# Glossary

**Accessories:** Miscellaneous and often expensive loose furnishings. Shop around for alternatives or wait to see if you actually need the items before investing top dollar for these. (Example: Parallax desk units, queuing stanchions.)

**ADA:** Americans with Disabilities Act (1990). Most state and local building codes should ensure compliance with ADA requirements, but it does not hurt to ask. Especially watch for space between stacks, basements or upper levels, and staff area requirements.

**Alcove:** Where the adult reference staff went when they fled the Nook (q.v.).

**Apology:** Used often and sincerely, will usually get you out of hot water and calm most anyone down. (Don't limit its use to building projects.)

**Architect:** Person or firm that designs the building. This person or firm (a) wants to win the design award, (b) wants to get in on the library boom and is practicing on yours, (c) can be your ally if you pay attention.

**Axonometric drawings:** Affectionately known as axons. Bird's-eye views of your future work space. See if you can talk your architect into a set of Colorforms to edit these.

**BAH:** Business after Hours. A Williamsburg Area Chamber of Commerce function (party). WRL used one to give chamber members a preview of JCCL, and two years later, to celebrate the completion of WL's renovation and parking.

**Books:** Used here, assume it means library materials including audio-visual.

**Branch:** What other systems might have termed JCCL. We did not, because neither of our primary funding municipalities wanted to be the location of a "branch."

**BS:** Catalog designation meaning "boxed storage." Honest.

**Bubble Machine:** Giant temporary air conditioner used at WL.

**Card Catalog:** Largely replaced by the computer catalogs. As of January 2000, WRL uses Dynix version 180. Includes bibliographic records and barcode holdings.

**Category 5 Cable:** Also as known as Cat5. High-end, versatile, and reliable cable that can handle networks and phone lines. Get it if you can. Subject to replacement by newer technologies, of course.

**CBI:** Crybaby issue. Don't waste everyone's time.

**CIP:** Cataloging-in-publication data usually found on the verso (back) of the title page.

**Circulation Department:** Used here, the check-out staff.

**Client:** Owner or user or both.

**Collection Services Department:** Used here, the check-in staff and security staff.

**Communication:** E-mail, voice, print, signs, whatever. Just keep using it.

**Construction Timetable:** While the expeditious building of floors, walls, windows, etc. is critical to the operation of your building, for the companies and people involved in constructing your facility, everything is "just another job, with just another timetable." Do not expect instant results because you asked for them in a nice way.

**Discount:** Mysterious term used by materials vendors. Treat with caution.

**Drive-up Book Drop:** Nice feature, but not used here.

**ETOP:** Extreme Temperature Operating Procedure.

**Expletive:** Pattern of speech the personnel manual says not to use; sometimes necessary to translate your request to a contractor.

**Future:** Close your eyes, imagine 20 years ahead, twice as much staff, four times the books. Now consider how much you can do without versus what the architect thinks you can do without.

**Giving Opportunities:** Examples include named meeting rooms, atlas stands, bricks, art, and books.

**Hot:** What the temperature is likely to be anytime you have a grand opening.

**HVAC:** Heating, Ventilation, and Air Conditioning. Get as long and as comprehensive a warranty as is available, even if you don't think you can afford it, and especially if you don't have a mechanical staff dedicated to its smooth operation. This isn't a copy machine you can stick giant tweezers in to fix.

**In-house:** Structural walls in which the public restrooms are enclosed at JCCL.

**ISP:** Internet Service Provider. You've heard of the big ones like America Online, but there are many more available now. Basically, the company or organization that sends you a bill for getting onto the Internet.

**JCCL:** James City County Library.

**Linux:** Network operating system and computer platform. Alternative to Windows NT. Free and relatively user-friendly. If you want to know more look it up.

**LMR:** Load MARC Records.

**Lunch Room:** Don't call it a lounge; it makes the staff sound lazy.

**MARC:** Machine-readable cataloging record.

**Mini-LAN:** The way WRL used it, it means a terminal server that split a single network cable connection into eight connections at the combined circulation/arts center desk.

**Modems:** Largely outdated technology, as far as libraries and other businesses are concerned, that did not become outdated until six months after JCCL was built. Sigh.

**Monolith:** Used here, the monolithic filing cabinets installed in the reference work room at JCCL.

**Naiveté:** What many WRL staff had before 1992. Now it's: cynicism.

**NB:** Catalog designation meaning New Building.

**Nook:** Reference work space used within TAFKATS.

**949 fields:** In the bibliographic records we purchased through our opening day collection vendor, "949 fields" were used to list each barcode attached to our new holding(s).

**OMR:** Output MARC Records.

**Owner:** Whoever pays the bills, usually a municipality.

**Patch cable:** The cable that goes between your equipment (computer, phone, etc.) and a wall jack.

**Pit:** Book and furniture storage area deep below WL.

**Project Coordinator:** Used here, the person hired by the owner to manage the project: for WL, the construction manager; for JCCL, the project manager.

**Project Engineer:** Construction management company "man on the scene." For JCCL, the county also had two "men on the scene."

**Project Executive:** Construction management company "boss."

**Project Liaison:** Used here, WRL's staff liaison to the architect(s) and contractor(s) for WL and JCCL.

**Proprietary:** New technology-related purchases that are proprietary will generally serve you well, but once they are not new anymore and need to be added to or upgraded, you're stuck buying your addendums or upgrades from the same manufacturer. That can mean higher expense and limitations. Try to stay away from proprietary stuff when you can so you'll have more choices down the road. In some cases, though, you're stuck, particularly with high-end network gizmos. But generally speaking, lean toward the more standard and less specific whenever possible.

**RFP:** Request for Proposal. Usually a package of specifications submitted to potential vendors. Done for big ticket items like an opening day collection, computers, furniture, and shelving, or whatever else your state or locality requires.

**Spray Paint:** One way to keep your staff amused while they deal with construction issues. Also try magnets, stickers, and gift certificates.

**Staff:** Will change frequently. Used here, library staff from custodian to director.

**Storage:** You know what it is. Ask for more.

**Tackable Surfaces:** Cork or other soft wallboard (usually under wallpaper) used for posters or exhibits. Architects sometimes mistake this for the long form of "tacky."

**TAFKATS:** The Area Formerly Known as Tech Services, a beehive into which virtually all off-desk staff activity went at WL.

**Technical Services:** Cataloging, acquisitions, etc.; at WRL, underwent a recent name change to Support Services.

**Telxons:** The portable inventory devices with attached barcode wands. WRL also uses them for check-out when the automated system server is down.

**Thanks:** Like an apology, usually appreciated and underused. Especially appropriate for use with construction professionals, staff who don't complain much, and directors.

**Turnkey:** Usually refers to a canned package of computer hardware and software, like a library web page template, or Internet access setup. Helpful to get your library or project going, especially if you have more money than staff expertise. Be sure to get the maintenance option so when the vendor changes the locks your key will still work.

**User:** Used here, from the architect or contractor's point of view: library director and staff.

**WL:** Williamsburg Library (building).

**WRL:** Williamsburg Regional Library (system).

# SECTION I

*Planning*

# 1

# Building New and
# Renovating Old

Getting a library built or renovated is often a time-consuming process. For Williamsburg Regional Library (WRL), the recognition that a second location was needed came as early as 1981, in James City County's long-range plan of that year. However, it took nearly ten years before any significant progress was made on the project. In 1990 WRL and James City County officials formed a committee to begin the property search for a James City County library. Committee members looked at parcels throughout the county. It took another four years to finalize plans to offer a bond referendum to fund the new James City County Library (JCCL). Construction on JCCL began in 1995, followed immediately by the Williamsburg Library (WL) expansion, which continued through April 1998.

For every construction project there are certain significant steps that are repeated, including preparing a building program, choosing an architect, reviewing blueprints, attending construction meetings, experiencing frustration, and (we hope) enjoying opening day. There are probably more similarities between building a new library and renovating an old one than there are differences. We maintain it is critically important in designing the most functionally effective building to involve all departments in the library.

## *James City County Library*

To inspire people to share new ideas, give opinions for decision making, or feel ownership for a new venture, we started with a staff meeting and invited everyone to participate. Long before JCCL was put out to bid, the staff of about 50 met to make plans for a new library to be built if and when funding was available. The director asked employees for ideas about desirable features for the new building and to consider ways such plans might be made into a real library building. Staff vision in no small way helped determine the end result.

Built new in an area that had no public building before, JCCL had no history to determine what it needed to look like, or how it was to function. Since the community had no preconceived notions of what the library should be, staff and architects were free to come up with a design based entirely on what they felt would create the most inviting surroundings for excellent library service.

One splendid advantage to building new is the flexibility to borrow design concepts from existing libraries. To this end, all staff were invited to travel in groups to other libraries to see how their designs worked. Staff members from every department made appointments to visit and photograph recently constructed libraries and see what worked and did not work for them. Site visits included Fayetteville and Chapel Hill, North Carolina, and Charlottesville, Chesapeake, Chinn Park, Fredericksburg, Loudoun County, Manassas, and Virginia Beach, Virginia. Staff also visited several large book stores to see what good ideas we could appropriate from the retail world. All of the sites had some appealing features, and staff were glad to see concrete examples of library construction rather than drawings and models. A favorite feature in the libraries we visited was ease of movement; that is, how some facilities almost take patrons by the hand and lead them through the library. Most accomplished this with clearly defined floor plans, excellent signs, and a friendly staff alert to the presence of patrons. Virtually all of these newer libraries had much better lighting than our older library did, and all of them seemed to have larger workrooms and staff areas.

While we learned what worked well, library staffs were eager to point out what did not work as well as they had thought it would. One library discovered the hard way that putting a computer room under a ceiling containing water pipes can have unfortunate repercussions. Some staff work rooms were awkwardly placed within the building or inefficiently arranged for the tasks to be performed. Some entrance areas were too large, overwhelming the patrons before they got into the library area, while others were too small, dark, or "busy," not inviting.

We were especially interested in the placement of the reference and information desk(s) and the placement of public restrooms. Staff also closely scrutinized circulation areas, including book returns. Exploring what other libraries had done sensitized staff to what we wanted to emphasize for JCCL. We sharpened our vision, added ideas, and noted solid examples.

The exterior of the James City County Library prior to signage application.

Examining what our peers were doing was, for staff, well worth the investment of time and money and we believe it paid off in the results we achieved
for the Williamsburg Regional Library system. Based on her previous experience and the visits to other libraries, WRL's director had a target size of
35,000 to 40,000 square feet in mind. County staff told her firmly that
voters in a bond referendum would support nothing larger than 25,000
square feet. The library board settled on 34,000 square feet at $6.1 mil-
lion, and the Friends of the Library spent the better part of a year lobbying for the referendum's passage. On March 1, 1994, the library referendum
passed with 78 percent of the vote, and the more tangible work began.
While the architect was designing the outside of the building, library staff
began examining workflow and planning for staffing. Many of us had never
worked in a system with more than one library building, so simulating desk
schedules for two buildings was a little surreal.

Building new also comes with its share of logistical complications.
Scheduling the delivery of equipment, furniture, and books in correct
order, late enough during construction to have everything in a climate
controlled environment but stored out of the way, is not easy. Add to the
formula the need to allow enough time to unpack, shelve, set up, and clean
up and the equation becomes truly daunting. Carefully select those who
will be faced with the problems of coordinating all of this. The successful

opening of a library is predicated on everything being ordered and received in a tight sequence, so the people making the ordering decisions and setting everything up need to be competent and motivated as well as empowered to make "field" decisions as quickly as necessary. The dedication of a new building should be a pleasurable experience for all in attendance. With planning and hard work it almost certainly can be.

## Williamsburg Library

Unlike the JCCL construction project, tremendous demands were placed on patrons and staff every day during the renovation and expansion of the Williamsburg Library from 28,000 square feet to 40,000 square feet. Some challenges stemmed from the decision, made early in the process, to remain open to the public as much as possible during the expansion project. Had we closed, renovation could have been completed more quickly, with construction personnel not having to circumnavigate library staff and patrons. It came down to this dilemma: Did we close and inconvenience the patrons by not allowing them access to Williamsburg Library at all? Or did we stay open and provide the best possible service under the circumstances and handle patron complaints about being inconvenienced by noise, limited parking, reduced access to books, power failures and other difficulties? We chose the latter, because in the case of WL, we were dealing with an existing building and an existing patronage, many of whom would have been most discomfited by giving up their library completely even for a few months — that is, wonderful, loyal library patrons.

Providing library service in a construction zone meant significantly increased stress on staff, especially at service desks. The renovation was a little like watching a caterpillar walk. It started at one end of the building, worked its way through the structure and then seemed to come back around. Plus, there was construction at the same time there was demolition. With most of the building under construction at one point or another in the process, library staff work spaces shifted repeatedly, public service desks moved (in the case of youth services, more than a mile from the building at one point), and books had to be stored and their unavailable status reflected in the catalog, then removed from storage and their status changed again.

The original WL building had many advantages. We had in-house storage space in the basement. This meant that moving various parts of the collection into and out of storage at various points was much less difficult than if storage had to be found off-site.

**The exterior of the Williamsburg Library after renovation.**

Since the James City County Library was completed before construction started at WL, we tried to schedule off-desk time as much at JCCL as possible. There were two reasons for this: (1) work space at WL was extremely limited, and (2) we wanted as little competition as possible between staff and public for parking areas, which shrank considerably when the construction fence went up. Something like a military operation, reference, circulation, and youth services staffs rotated up to the front lines at the WL construction site and then away from the combat zone to JCCL. After a week to a month in the relative calm of JCCL the staff returned to the trenches, refreshed and ready for the mission to continue to provide the best possible library service in the midst of a major construction project.

For several years before the start of the two construction projects, WRL had been closed to the public on Fridays. We chose the slowest day of the week to close, to allow staff to concentrate on less public aspects of public service: collection development, staff training and departmental meetings, and outreach such as school story times. While vital to the ongoing business of the library before construction, having one day per week that the library was already closed proved to be a godsend during construction. Friday became a day for projects that needed to be completed in public areas; with no patrons and few staff around, construction workers could lay carpet and rewire areas without great danger or inconvenience to anyone.

A new building under construction elicits some attention from those who drive by. An existing building that is being renovated while it is opened to the public draws a flood of inquiries. For this reason the public relations associated with the renovations were far more extensive than with the new building. WL patrons received regular progress reports as well as anticipated changes in library hours. We included information in the local newspapers, the library's monthly newsletter, on our web pages and through flyers and displays in the library. We wanted to keep patrons as informed as possible, as far in advance of inconvenience as possible. At least then when a patron asked "How long before the noise stops?" over the roar of a jack hammer, a staff member could give an answer and provide a copy of the projected construction timetable.

All libraries no doubt have an active program of communication with the public. A library's public includes those who depend, or who may depend, on the library for service as well as those on whom the library depends, or on whom it may depend, for funding and support. Communicating with these constituencies is a vital part of library management, and becomes even more crucial during the changes a renovation brings.

What is sometimes less obvious than the need to communicate is the best method of communicating with these sometimes dissimilar groups. At WRL we focused on how to communicate with patrons, those who depended on the library for service. They were the people, outside of library staff, who would be most affected by the turmoil that occurs during a construction project. As it turned out, reaching them was not as hard as we anticipated.

During the renovation of WL, library staff used a variety of methods to notify the public about changes and disruptions that would occur. First among them were news releases and public service announcements (PSAs). These are standard methods that libraries use to get information out to the media. Libraries are in a wonderful position to get free "advertising" for their products and services; newspapers and electronic media do not tend to view a library as cautiously as they do a commercial or political organization that sends a news release. Some media outlets such as public television and radio are required to actively help promote community organizations, so these are natural targets for any publicity efforts.

Two publications for sale through the American Library Association that have the benefit of not being over long are *Part-Time Public Relations with Full-Time Results: A PR Primer for Libraries* and *Programming Author*

*Visits.* Another excellent source of information is the American Library Association Public Information web site (http://www.ala.org/pio/index. html). Any of these guides would help a library structure a communications strategy.

Knowing where and to whom to send releases is also an important part of the publicity effort. In addition to contact names you already have, staff have found that publications like the Gale Research, Inc. *Directory of Publications and Broadcast Media* provide fax numbers of the media that serve your area. General releases can be addressed simply to the "Editor" for publications and "News Director" for electronic media (TV and radio). At larger newspapers, program announcements can be directed to specific editors, who can be identified by calling the paper. Program announcements should also be directed to the "Calendar Editor," the person who compiles the laundry list of events going on in your community. Using a computer and the fax software that comes bundled with most modems can be an easy and cost effective method of getting the word out to many media outlets at once. Many media now use e-mail as well, and Gale's will often list e-mail addresses for publications and electronic media.

Included in any news release are standard components of who, what, when, where, why, and how. There is no reason to worry about making your release a literary masterpiece. The facts speak for themselves. Most of the time the publication or program will rework a release to fit its available space or time anyway. At WRL we have found that sending a photo with information included as a caption is a very effective way to get the word out.

WRL is fortunate enough to have a graphics manager to design posters and signs that are creative and informative. If your library is as fortunate, great. But if not, do not despair. There are many fine computer programs that range in price and ease of use that can render very professional looking posters and flyers. Some amazingly professional products can be created with relatively little effort by staff. And, you might find that staff from multiple departments are interested in this kind of artistic venture.

At WRL we kept people up to date using all the standard methods. Each time there was something of consequence to report, we did. We also made sure to periodically issue more comprehensive updates for patrons and staff alike. When phone numbers changed during construction we printed bookmarks and then magnets with the new library numbers. The effort did not reach every patron, but it was a start.

We made a special effort to publicize how to connect to WRL's catalog from a personal computer, in order to provide an effective alternative to making patrons wade through the turmoil of construction to find out whether the library owned a particular book. When foot traffic was rerouted around construction obstructions, staff enjoyed painting footprints directly onto the soon-to-be-replaced carpet to direct the way. One of the temporary construction walls at WL was covered with butcher paper. We then used the paper as a billboard and spray painted directions and information on it. At one point we also invited local children to draw and paint pictures on large pages and then used the temporary wall for a giant display of their art. It was a wonderful way to make an otherwise unappealing floor to ceiling particle board wall interesting, amusing, and pleasant.

WRL also made use of our web site to the fullest possible extent in advertising the latest construction updates. By developing a section on our homepage with just construction news, we gave patrons with access to the Internet a great source of information about the renovation. It was updated regularly, sometimes daily, and included photos of the construction site as it progressed, the architect's rendering of the finished building, floor plans, and construction news. We posted the construction timeline as well as contact information for questions about different aspects of the project; we posted similar information on bulletin boards inside the library. It was only fair to keep the public well informed on the progress of the entire project — they were paying for it.

Finally, the program services director found a wealth of information by joining the ALA-sponsored PRTalk e-mail list. He could find out from other library professionals and public relations experts around the country what has worked for them. (To subscribe, send message to: listproc@ ala.org. Leave the subject blank. In the body of the message, type: subscribe PRTalk your first and last name.) Most library people enjoy sharing their expertise with someone in need.

# 2

# Building New

After a parcel of wooded land was chosen in 1994 for the new James City County Library, the real work began for library staff. Just building on a previously undeveloped lot provided a challenge. There was a brief flurry of comments from citizens worried about the impending destruction of the trees on the lot. To encourage community participation, staff arranged for a public meeting in July of 1994 in Norge, the town nearest to the new library. Citizens saw a model of the new library, and library staff, the architect, and the project engineer answered questions. As it turned out, there were few concerns expressed at the meeting. Most of the community's residents attended to convey happy anticipation of their new library.

While WRL staff was also happily anticipating the new building, wrangling over architectural designs posed special challenges for us. Each library department shared the experience of planning its area at JCCL, each encountering its own obstacles, frustrations, and benefits. The lessons staff learned within departments were not department specific. The importance of details, understanding, communication, and compromise repeatedly appeared in assorted incarnations. As an institution we learned that if we did not remain dynamically involved in the construction process, we would lose our ability to influence the progress of the construction project. Conversely, when we remained involved, we found that we could help the architect to think more creatively, and vice versa, like friendly adversaries.

Automatic doors might not be creative or new in the world, but to us they were exciting. JCCL has two parallel sets of automatic doors that form the entranceway, and they are much appreciated by patrons carrying large stacks of books. Between these automatic doors are the interior book drops. We labeled each for a different material format, an idea we got from touring a new library in Chesapeake, Virginia. To the surprise and pleasure of our collection services department, patrons observe the "Adult," "Children's," and "Media" (we'll change that eventually to "A/V") signs, making sorting easier and faster. We also found that providing a shallow shelf along the front of the book drops is a convenience patrons enjoy. It gives them a place to put belongings down while they take off coats or sort through types of books and put them in slots. The area also proved to be useful for a tackable surface to display community announcements and flyers.

A single floor building, JCCL has drawn comments from patrons on its feeling of openness. With a ceiling over 25 feet high and few interior walls in the public areas, the building is sectioned by book classification rather than physical structure. A primary concern for JCCL was flexibility in design, since that had never been an option at WL. At WL, the downstairs book stacks were constructed as part of the support structure for the upstairs, so the central core of book stacks cannot be moved.

A word about planning for the future is in order here. Be prepared to stand your ground about the flexibility you want in a floor plan, computer and telephone cabling, furniture arrangements and wall covering, or anything else you need. You will be questioned by the architect, the architect's engineers, and probably others. During our pre-construction travels, we often heard the refrain, "We didn't want it this way, but the architect insisted." Staff must stand up for what they need; library staff understand function, architects understand aesthetics. Rarely is it wise to let aesthetics rule at the expense of function and efficient operations.

## JCCL Floor Plan

When a patron comes in the entrance to JCCL, he enters at the middle of the building. To his left are the new book and video display areas, the Friends book sale area, public restrooms, and 175–person meeting room. Beyond the Friends sale shelves, is the youth services department comprising at least half of the public space at JCCL. Straight ahead from the entrance are the reference desk, two 15–person meeting rooms, and all the adult book and periodical stacks. To the patron's right are the copier room and computer room, the quiet study room, and the check-out desk. Beyond the check-out desk is a door leading to the staff workrooms.

Signage consists of a few large, simple signs hung from the ceiling directing patrons to various parts of the library, most of which are in view immediately upon entering the building. The signs in the reference, adult stack, and check-out areas are painted to coordinate with trim on the service desks and with the carpet, and ornamented with small geometric shapes of brushed aluminum and cherry colored wood. The print is white, in a clean, modern font. In the youth services area, most of the signs are large primary-colored arrows, reminiscent of curved crayons. Youth services staff actually hit upon this idea while doodling during an otherwise unproductive meeting about signs.

In the new book and audio-video shelving, which we call the New and Notable area, we placed brightly cushioned benches near the wall-height windows in the corner. Adjacent to the 175–person meeting room, called the Community Room, is a full-service kitchen, and there is a short antechamber where a sign-in table can be set up.

To prevent the restrooms from being too prominent, architects enclosed them in a semicircular set of walls that acts as a de facto separation between youth services and adult services. The walls of this "in-house" turned out to be quite useful for displays as well. Between the doors to the two restrooms is a drinking fountain and a tackable wall area.

The approach to the youth services department houses a modular station with three computers known as the Family Computer Literacy Center, and a large colorful book drop disguised as a train engine. At the rear of the public restroom "building" is the Teen, Etc. section, which also serves as the thruway to the adult area. Staff discussed the pros and cons of providing doors between adult and youth services, and opted instead to use the young adult shelving to shield potentially noisy sections (i.e., the toddler area), which were placed toward the rear of youth services to distance them from the adult areas. This is an innovation which has worked well; rarely does excessive noise from youth services interfere with patrons using the adult area.

## *Youth Services*

JCCL is a very child-friendly library. Youth services, including staff work areas, represent nearly a third of JCCL's square footage. Much of the shelving is modular, which is attractive and has the advantage of flexibility. One disadvantage is the shelving looks like ladders to small children. Occasionally, little patrons try to climb up the sides of the shelving or onto the moveable shelves. Somewhere there is a shelving system with a more perfect balance of flexibility and stability, but we haven't seen it yet.

As library professionals, youth services staff spends much of their time finding out what WRL's young patrons want and need. We spend the rest of our time meeting those needs as best we can. It is a team effort, with storytellers, collections specialists, and administrators all dedicated to the goal. Likewise, we understood that we could not build a library or expand and renovate one without an assembly of specialized construction professionals: an architect, an interior designer, engineers, and so on. We believed that they would listen to us and do their best to meet our needs and expectations (as we do for patrons), since we were the clients. That did not always prove to be true.

The youth services department experienced first hand how construction professionals can work around library professionals, rather than with them. The construction professionals claimed greater expertise in the construction arena while sometimes ignoring staff expertise in the library environment. Following are a few examples.

Children's librarians covet tackable walls to easily and temporarily display children's art, program announcements, posters and an array of other resources. Youth services staff planned JCCL display walls carefully to provide tackable wall areas that could be used sensibly without dominating the space. Although the plans were drawn up in consultation with the architects and designers, the final results in JCCL (and WL) differed from the concepts the staff originally discussed with the designers.

It was not until nearly opening day that we discovered what we had specified was not what we received. When experts hung the wallpaper a few days before the grand opening at JCCL, we discovered that about 50 percent of our anticipated tackable space was not tackable. When staff checked the blueprints we discovered that half of the tackable surfaces we had discussed with the architect had been eliminated from the final drawings. We had stressed the importance of tackable surfaces early and often with the architect, and it never occurred to us that our preferences would not be respected. However, when asked about the loss of tackable wall space, the architect admitted it had not appealed to his sense of aesthetics. He had concluded that all that tackable space would make it too easy for library staff to hang garish exhibits; so without consulting library staff, he modified the plans.

The director of youth services realized after the fact that she should have paid more attention to the blueprints. This kind of detail illustrates why, in addition to a project liaison, representatives from other departments would do well to stay involved. Looking back, there was forewarning about the architect's intentions had the youth services director recognized it. At the public meeting about JCCL, she noticed that the plans and renderings showed picture book shelving with peaked canopies designed to display a few tastefully selected picture books. When she asked about the utility of the canopies in the sketch, he replied that he preferred that type of canopy top on low shelving so that children's staff could not clutter the shelving with bric-a-brac. A further clue to his willingness to disregard our preferences came when the youth services director reminded him that she was the children's librarian who would presumably be doing the cluttering. He did not blink an eye. Although JCCL avoided the peaked canopies, the architect did have his way on the tackable surfaces.

Because we are notorious pack rats, children's librarians also need storage space. We store colored paper, fuzzy puppets, summer reading incentives in all shapes and sizes, and a cornucopia of other supplies. With that in mind, we asked for and received generous storage rooms at JCCL. That space includes a storage cabinet we intended to hold posters, poster board, construction paper, paints, and a medley of craft supplies. We love the cabinet's drawer space, but the people who constructed it had no concept of the weight of paper. After only three months of use the bottoms were falling out of the drawers. Construction folks kindly repaired the drawer bottoms by adding braces, but they warned us to be more careful about how much we put in the unreinforced drawers. We have not quite figured out how to use a five foot high, eight foot long cabinet that was not designed to hold the weight of craft supplies. If there is a next time we will know to investigate the weight tolerance of storage units.

Our experiences in youth services underscore why it is important to be involved in every step of the construction process. Without question, it proves time consuming to keep abreast of all the architectural and construction details. But this learning experience will make the end product better. An additional lesson we learned is you should attempt to include financial penalties for the architect or other construction professionals if at all possible. Because there will always be mistakes or omissions, intentional and not, you'll want to have some recourse beyond the construction team's good word.

## *Adult Reference*

The adult reference desk is centrally located, with line of sight to both the youth services and check-out desks. Reference staff can easily direct patrons to the youth services desk, the check-out desk or the restroom simply by motioning, so staff believe the location is nearly ideal. Most of the staff's effort went into designing the desk space itself.

Design of the desk proved challenging because the entire reference department was vitally concerned with the desk design and all revisions of the desk design. The staff who work that desk are pleased with the end result, fortunately. Front and back counters are at standing height, the third side counter accommodates shelving for patron requests and reference resources, and the fourth side has a regular desk-height counter, allowing librarians a place to work and still be at the reference desk when library traffic is slow, in addition to providing an accessible service area for the disabled.

The reference desk would have taken much less time to design had an early deadline been set for revisions or a smaller committee, rather than the department as a whole, been entrusted with the design features. That department felt that getting agreement from the entire staff was important to designing the most effective service desk. Other departments found, however, that unlimited discussion on every consideration simply slowed the process too much. In addition, reaching for consensus on every issue can sometimes lead to unrealistic decisions; for example, at one point the reference desk was slated to have four incoming telephone lines when the desk was likely, at maximum, to be staffed with three librarians. In other departments, one spokesperson with decision making power would keep his or her co-workers informed and make overall management of the project much easier.

Inspired by the larger retail book stores as well as the libraries we toured, we sought to make JCCL as attractive and comfortable as possible. Toward that end, the architect included a small reading area we refer to as the solarium. With floor to ceiling windows, this 20 square foot area is like a large bay window extending into the surrounding woods, but with a ceiling height much lower than the rest of the library. Patrons love to take books and magazines back there to read in relatively cozy surroundings. We furnished it with comfortable chairs and ottomans, and it gets morning sun so it's not uncomfortably warm. We also have study tables positioned between the windowed rear wall of the library and the last range of shelving for people who want a more secluded area in which to read. With cherry wood paneling, tables and shelving, the entire area has a touch of elegance while remaining warm and inviting.

Although the solarium is usually quiet, we did include an enclosed quiet study room based on use at the original WL. The JCCL quiet study room can accommodate 30 to 40 people. This is one of the two areas in which we "overbuilt" because of inadequacies at the existing WL. Patrons at the very small, very busy WL consistently complained about noise, so when we had a chance to build a brand new library, we wanted a large quiet study area. However, the overall design for JCCL makes it a quieter building, so people rarely need the quiet study area for quiet study. We are now considering converting the area into a computer lab for staff and public training.

Along the wall to the right of the adult reference desk are an enclosed room for copiers, a small room for word processing, and a room intended for private reference interviews— all visible from the adult reference desk. The interview room was rarely used, and turned out to be a wonderful space for the Phillip West Memorial Cancer Resource Center (www.west-cancer.org), a project developed by WRL reference staff with funding from the West family through the Williamsburg Community Hospital. The rooms in the public areas of JCCL were designed with specific purposes, but we kept the built-ins to a minimum so that room uses can change along with library services. There is enough space remaining in the copier room for a third machine if needed; however, when library staff recently received approval from the library board to allow beverages in the library, they discovered that copier space can easily accommodate a soda machine.

The word processing room required special attention in its design, since it was a new initiative that the construction of JCCL made possible. The adult reference staff championed public computers for word processing from the very beginning of the planning process for JCCL. It fell to the online technology librarian and the business/government librarian to work on designing and implementing this feature of the new building. The generosity of Robert and Jane G. McGaw, loyal library supporters and donors (Mr. McGaw is also a long-term volunteer), made possible the equipping of the public computing and word processing room.

Reference librarians decided that the computers should be located near the reference desk for troubleshooting purposes. They suggested that the room be large enough to contain six computers: three per wall with each trio sharing a printer. When the final blueprints were completed, modular furniture was selected for the space, which holds three computers, two printers, and a typewriter. The furniture can be reconfigured to add one more workstation if needed. Staff also specified a locked supply cabinet for the room.

Since most of our patrons use IBM–compatible machines but the local schools used Macintosh computers, staff decided to purchase two personal computers and one Macintosh. A typewriter was donated by a local government office and is used primarily by patrons who need to fill out forms and applications. A laser printer is shared by the two PCs to ensure high quality printouts for those producing resumes and cover letters. A color printer for flyers and children's projects is attached to the Macintosh.

Staff spoke to the technology coordinator for the local schools and purchased the same Macintosh software that they used: ClarisWorks and At Ease (a security program). For the PCs they chose Corel WordPerfect Suite and Microsoft Office, since WordPerfect and Word were the most popular word processing software packages. The suite versions provided the most utility to those patrons who would need spreadsheets and drawing programs. Staff tried a number of different PC security software packages before finding one that worked fairly well; however, the search for better security programs continues. While the word processing machines are not attached to the library's network, the room was wired for data lines in anticipation of networking the computers in the future. So far, however, the potential security problems of networking public machines continue to dissuade us from changing the independent installations.

Originally we thought we would have money to purchase various CD-ROMs for patrons to use in the public computer room. After we opened JCCL, however, adult reference staff did not feel we had enough money to create an effective collection, and there are still no plans to support such acquisitions. Staff also felt that the demand for word processing might be so high that the CD-ROMs would not get much use. And in fact the use of word processing computers has been very high.

Troubleshooting the computers falls to adult reference staff, with assistance from members of the automated services department when problems prove too technical. Reference staff held a few training sessions before the library opened; however, most of the learning occurred and continues to occur during the course of the working day. Software manuals as well as a dictionary and thesaurus are shelved in the word processing room for patrons to consult. Reference staff help patrons as time permits, but assistance is necessarily minimal. Volunteers have been solicited to help train patrons on word processing software, but their numbers remain quite small. Patrons can sign up at the reference desk when they want to use the computers. We currently take reservations up to a day ahead of time for two-hour sessions.

Another staff-designed area was the circulation (check-out) desk. The only trouble we experienced with our design on this desk was forgetting to include a place for the cash register. Luckily we caught this omission before construction was completed and a quick modification to the counter top made room for the register. The interior designer also jazzed up the modular counter by adding a 45–degree brightly painted panel to hide the backs of computer monitors. It is a bit reminiscent of an informal bank setup and includes easy staff access from both ends of the counter.

In front of the circulation counter we planned a queuing counter inspired by one in a local post office. Two notable lessons came from that design. With a fun-house mirror that runs the length of the counter from floor to about 30 inches, toddlers are more apt to stay with their beleaguered parents than run off. This is great fun for staff to watch too. If you try a fun-house mirror, be sure it's designed to be flush with the top of the counter, or just adhere it to the face of the desk. Our counter extends three to four inches over the mirror, like a small awning, where taller children occasionally hit their heads. Heavy brushed aluminum queuing stanchions effected more trouble than queue management; and besides that they were expensive. Small patrons quickly discovered that by hanging on the velvet ropes they could bring a stanchion down on themselves. We switched to lightweight plastic ones for safety and ease of use, then abandoned them altogether in favor of a counter top sign that says "line forms here."

Having the reference desk in view of the circulation desk simplifies referring patrons from one desk to the other. It certainly works better than trying to convey directions or handing a patron a diagram of the floor plan. In addition, there are obvious safety features when staff are able to see each other and the only public entrance all at the same time. Patrons also seem to enjoy and use the clear views in the library; they can see when there's a line at either desk and will pace themselves until the queue is shorter.

Furnishings in the public areas of JCCL lean toward the modern but comfortable side of aesthetics, including the furniture in the large community meeting room and two smaller meeting rooms. The meeting room chairs and tables are attractive; unfortunately, each table weighs well over 50 pounds and they were pricey as well. The weight of the tables makes self-service meeting room adjustments by patrons nearly impossible and requires that staff are either relatively strong or that they enlist the help of others to arrange tables. While staying in good shape is a noble cause, we never intended to contribute to that goal by offering a weight-lifting program.

## *Staff Workrooms*

The majority of the behind-the-scenes work at JCCL occurs in the wing of the building accessible through a door behind the check-out desk, where most of the departments have staff workrooms. The JCCL staff area is a series of rooms along a wide corridor. The staff entrance and loading dock is on one end, and the door to the public areas is on the other. From the loading dock, down one side is the mail room, technical services, supply closet, staff conference room, automated services office and computer room, and circulation workroom. This side of the hall fronts the parking lot so technical services staff can spot patrons' cars burning up and the circulation director can panic when a school bus pulls up to the front door. From the loading dock down the other side is the bookmobile office, janitor's closet, staff lunchroom, staff restroom, graphics workroom, and the adult reference workroom. This side is on the rear of the building with a nice view of the trees, including two dogwoods donated by a local garden club.

One advantage of this single hallway is that it centralizes the entire behind-the-scenes operation. We can leave messages that will be seen as staff enter the library (for example, "the network is down"; "JJ's leaving her car in the parking lot over the weekend"). Once inside, the flow of the hallway allows efficiency-minded staff members to develop a nice routine: check snail mail, put away a lunch, check the fax machine, see what's going on in departments and then settle in at one's desk.

An amazing number of considerations beyond departmental layout went into designing the staff only areas. Things that seemed mundane turned out to have hidden benefits. For a small example, the restroom is unisex, with a vacant/occupied lock as on airplanes. A nice feature of the lock has turned out to be that someone with good eyes can tell from down the hall if the restroom is occupied (red). The janitor's closet compensates for its shallow depth with double doors so staff can have access to all the contents, as if it were a huge kitchen pantry. The closet includes a sink, and a drain in the floor, industrial shelves on one end for paper supplies, and hooks for spray bottles. Located next to the staff kitchen area, it is in a high traffic area, so the corridor was made wide enough to allow access to the lunchroom even when the closet doors are open.

A relaxed atmosphere was an important feature of the staff lunchroom. Set up a little like a cafe, the lunchroom seats 12 (at three tables) and a few more on a love seat without feeling crowded. There is plenty of room for a snack machine, soda machine, sink, cabinets, a microwave oven and refrigerator with an ice maker. There is a nice view of the woods behind the library, and the windows open to air out unexpected popcorn burns and fishy lunches.

When designing JCCL, WRL staff wanted a garage for the bookmobile and a workroom for bookmobile staff. If you have the space and budget, a bookmobile garage is a good investment. The bookmobile manager has her own office with a small window facing the parking lot. There are two workstations in the workroom, six ranges of shelves, and a door leading to the garage. As we have repeatedly discovered, storage space is of some concern in this area, even if bookmobile staff are too good-tempered to complain. It is rare that enough storage is actually built into a facility, and JCCL is no exception. The garage looks cavernous because clearance needs of the bookmobile dictated a tall space; however, there is not room for more than book carts around the bookmobile itself. JCCL has virtually no "ugly" storage; for example, to store boxes of books for a Friends sale or a broken chair until it's repaired.

The graphics workroom is home to the graphics manager, who handles the library's press releases, newsletter, signs, bookmark and name tag orders, and works on our website. This space also is the central workroom for staff photocopying, faxing, paper cutting, and laminating. This is an efficient location for everyone but the graphics manager. Due to her proximity and her graciousness, she has become an expert on the library's shared equipment. The graphics workroom does boast long counter tops and kitchen style cabinets filled with art supplies to accommodate creative projects, and of course enough floor space to work on really big projects.

We have a custom-designed set of shelves, drawers, and cabinets in this room to house different sized papers, public relations archives, and other mysterious tools of the talented. This is one of the few workrooms in the building that has sufficient storage space, by virtue of its size and relative lack of furniture. JCCL's limited storage is a good illustration of how quickly a new building's space can fill up, in the design process as well as once it opens for business.

There is a relatively large storage closet at JCCL that holds office supplies, tax forms, copy paper, receipt printer paper sometimes, and whatever else anyone throws in there. We joke that this central storage closet will be someone's office someday. When office space becomes more precious than storage space, it probably will be.

A room that started out as probable branch head office space on the plans is the staff conference and training room. We would probably include the staff meeting room again since it is extremely convenient for meetings of the library's governing board, staff evaluations, employment interviews and other meetings in which privacy or quiet is useful. Its capacity is 15 to 18 comfortably seated, with more seating space along two walls. Hung on the walls are white boards. These are movable, like track lighting. The other piece of furniture in the room is a credenza that neatly stores coffee and paper supplies.

Across the hall from the staff conference room are the automated services workroom and the computer room. In library land, as elsewhere, automated services has blossomed into an indispensable library function for patrons and staff alike. At WRL, the department has grown to a systems administrator, a network administrator, and two full-time computer technicians. Although the whole team troubleshoots at both library buildings, the two administrators share the JCCL workroom space with various manuals, spare parts, and an occasional experimental server. The two technicians have space in both buildings: one in the graphics workroom at JCCL and one off the youth services workroom at WL. As the library's services expand through the use of computers and the Internet, automated services staff are confronted with incorporating these resources into library buildings. So naturally our automated services staff were involved daily in the intricacies of construction. For WRL, the process of network planning for the new building and for the one to be renovated followed similar paths; that is, starting from the ground up. At WL the network infrastructure ("infrastructure" means wiring and wall plates, for us technophobes) was so outdated and patched together, and so tangled with 15 years' worth of telephone and electrical wiring additions, that complete replacement was the only reasonable option.

We'll digress here into several pages of geek-speak, so if you're not reading this at home in bed, we won't be offended if you flip forward a few pages to the next workroom section.

Before architects began work, departments reviewed their existing and projected work patterns to determine the number and type of workstations to request for each office and public use area. This information was used by architects to configure work spaces and by the library's automated services staff to determine specific equipment needed for each location. Once plans were drawn, automated services staff and the library's project liaison examined the blueprints space by space and marked the locations for and numbers of power, network, voice, and data connections required. Knowing that space usage changes over time to accommodate expanding staff and new missions, we positioned connections not only to serve stated needs for each area, but also to allow for alternate configurations of the space. Permit us to mention again that you should be prepared to defend why, for example, you want to lay computer cable to the quiet study room or put power receptacles in the supply closet. At departmental meetings, management team meetings, construction meetings, and lunches, we brainstormed about how this room or that corner might one day be used. Although it sounds like pure speculation, the fact that we had by that time upwards of 80 employees crammed into a 28,000 square foot building made future scenarios easier to envision.

Adding JCCL to our library system through new construction meant creating a new network environment. Our rudimentary in-house-only system consisted of dumb terminals connected directly to an Ultimate 3040 main frame computer, with no dial-in and certainly no Telnet access. The new network would supplant it with a mix of PCs and dumb terminals in two buildings, accessing our library's automated system through terminal servers and hubs connected to a Hewlett-Packard 9000 server housed in a specially designed computer room located at JCCL. A T-1 circuit would provide a connection between the buildings. The size of the new library facility required that cabling there be installed in two sections, one terminating in the computer room and the other in a repeater room halfway across the building.

And here, unfortunately, is where we need to digress further into a short discussion on network protocols and the speed of light. How far one is able to send network data via regular copper wires greatly depends on the type of network you have. We chose to set up an Ethernet network and this type has a length limitation of 300 feet — if you use copper wire. Because our buildings are over 300 feet long, we chose to cover the distance by having two rooms with copper wire in them, and link these two rooms with fiber optic cable, which sends data at speeds approaching the speed of light. This type of cable, requiring special and not inexpensive interfaces in each room, is not subject to the 300–foot limitation like copper wire. The effect is that although these rooms are hundreds of feet apart, as far as the Ethernet network is concerned they are right next to each other.

This configuration later allowed us to open our system to the Internet. Design of our new network and purchase and installation of supporting network equipment was handled largely under a maintenance contract with Ameritech Library Services, which was then the provider of our Dynix automated library system. Lesson learned: use all your resources and contacts whenever you can.

We chose to handle the conversion process in stages. A year before opening JCCL, we migrated from our Ultimate mainframe to the HP server. (In the nick of time, too; the Ultimate literally went up in flames as we were transferring files. Another story for another time....) The hardware migration, in our existing building, resulted in the installation of the first elements of the network infrastructure — terminal servers and hubs to connect dumb terminals and PCs to the automated catalog server. Completing this migration before putting other elements in place gave staff, automated services included, the chance to adjust to new logins and procedures before moving on to the next phase.

Changes caused by construction ran the gamut. Logins might seem like a small addition to the daily routine, but they added a step that affected every staff member. That sort of universal change causes a reaction that can be positive or negative, and typically will be a mix. Similarly, the equipment assessments and wish lists for any construction project probably involve staff (or at least departments) collectively. At the same time, few WRL staff truly understood why automated services kept drawing us little pictures of what the new network would look like.

Long before opening day at JCCL, each department had charted its workflow and identified as best it could what adjustments would be needed to handle two sites. Out of this review came departmental requests for the number of workstations, the type of equipment needed for each workstation and any specialized computer software needed. The library's management team, made up of department directors, selected core software for use on all new PCs — Windows 95 as the operating system, Corel Suite 7 for office functions, Calendar Creator and Norton AntiVirus. (Another aside here: As with some of the equipment we ordered, the software package choice was something of a catch–22. At the time, Microsoft Office was just coming into prominence. In retrospect it probably would have been better to make the switch from Corel.) Using this information, automated services drafted a profile of each workstation — the type of terminal required (PC or dumb terminal); the specifications for each PC; peripherals required, such as barcode reader, receipt printer, desktop printer, modem, spine label printer; and what software would be needed. Four distinct specification profiles were developed for workstations: public service desk terminal (dumb terminals), basic PC workstation (staff use), Internet PC workstation (public use), CD workstation (public use). Additional specifications were developed for printers: a public area printer and a basic PC workstation printer. The profiles were used when putting out equipment lists for bid. The profiles gave us the ability to accurately compare the value of bid packages and to be sure that essential specification requirements were being met. Specifications for PCs included the type and speed of the central processing unit (CPU), amount of RAM, type of network card, and size of the hard drive. Also included was the number of serial ports and expansion bays, so we could be assured that connection ports would be available for all peripherals needed at each workstation. See Appendix C for more information on the specification sheets. Spreadsheets divided by department and area of the building detailed what equipment went where and what software needed to be installed on each machine. This level of organization proved useful as a means to track all the information about computer equipment in one place.

Six months before opening day, equipment lists, complete with specification profiles, were ready to bid, so we forwarded them to the county purchasing office. The building plan called for the county purchasing department to handle the bidding and purchase of all equipment not coming from sole source vendors.

Flexibility in procedures and the ability to adapt to change undoubtedly prove to be important components to keeping any construction project on track. The cliché "expect the unexpected" has substance to it when we review some of the amazing turns and twists that were experienced during the construction of JCCL. The bidding process is a prime example of an operation beyond the control of library staff. A month before opening day, we discovered that no bid packets had been released and no equipment, other than from sole source vendors, had been ordered. This meant no PCs or display terminals through which our library system would be accessed had been purchased. A contingency plan was immediately executed in which the library's purchasing agent prepared bid packets and assumed responsibility for ordering equipment. Since there was not sufficient time to have all equipment bid, ordered and in place by opening day, equipment was prioritized. High-visibility public service areas were equipped first. Most public service workstations were to be dumb terminals that could be purchased at the highest savings under state contract; this procedure identified the vendor offering the lowest price and assured delivery within a month. These workstations were ordered and were the only terminals available for the first month of the new building's operation, with the exception of four leased CD-ROM workstations delivered an hour before the first patrons entered the building. Fortunately, lightpens and receipt printers had been purchased through sole source vendors, so most public service desk workstations had good functionality. Reference searching capabilities were limited to our own database until PCs with modem connections to outside search sources could be delivered and installed. A month after opening, PCs, printers and database CD-ROM workstations began to arrive, allowing us to complete the set up of staff offices and workrooms and public access to CD-ROM and outside databases.

Like the public areas and computer room around the adult reference desk, the reference department's workroom at JCCL was well designed except for what became known as the Monolith. The office has nice windows overlooking the woods, good lighting, and one cubicle for every two librarians. Because all our public service staff split their time between the two library buildings, each cubicle can be assigned to two people. When one partner is at JCCL the other is at WL, so there is rarely a conflict of office space (they also have a shared cubicle at WL). This has worked well for us. The Monolith, however, is a different story.

When we first opened the building, we were obligated to take delivery of a significantly taller storage cabinet than the plans specified. Staff intended to have a bank of filing units that would run down the center of the room, positioned to provide convenient access from the flanking cubicles as well as a broad working surface. When originally installed, the units were stacked to a height of three rather than the correct two units shown on the furnishings plan. Christened "the Monolith," the files were unusable and also impeded communication across the office by even the tallest members of the staff. It was like having a rectangular granite mountain in the middle of the reference workroom. With few mountain climbing enthusiasts in the department, it was not used during the many months it took for the supplier to correct the installation. The corrected cabinets and lateral files are great, fortunately, offering good storage and counter space and serving as an informal gathering table and a place to find cookies or saltwater taffy after somebody's vacation.

Since the reference librarians work in both buildings and share desk space, it was prudent to include a bank of flipper door "lockers" in each library, to provide some personal space for each librarian. Flipper door units (we also call them "cubbies") are essentially shelves with end panels and a miniature sliding garage door. The door can be upholstered to match a decor, and the unit itself comes in standard sizes from modular furniture vendors. The lockers we use are 24 inches wide by 18 inches tall by 12 inches deep. As numbers of staff have increased, locking units for each staff member have been added to the original bank of lockers. We used flipper door units for private storage in other workrooms as well.

The circulation workroom is JCCL's largest workroom, divided about evenly between check-out staff work area and check-in staff work area. The interior walls have ranges of sorting shelves. Because we sort children's materials and videos directly to carts, we do not need much sorting space. There is enough desk space for typewriters (typing address labels, library card envelopes, and assorted other typing jobs for which a computer is not suitable), counting the previous day's cash register till, word processing, answering the telephone, and checking in books. One aspect of the design that has worked nicely is that the interior and exterior book drops both empty into closets in the workroom. That convenience means no transporting of books from a book drop outside or at the other end of the building, except for some children's books that are returned in a small drop in the children's area. And since the materials drop into enclosed closets, instead of directly into the work area, noise is not a significant problem.

Early in the planning process, staff urged the architect to devise a drive-up book drop. Library staff and the architect wanted a drive-up book drop that emptied into the building, rather than a free-standing box requiring a trip outside to empty it. We were certain that our 14–acre lot would allow sufficient space to accommodate such a wonderful convenience for patrons. However, our lot is longer than it is wide. To position a drive-up book drop with the drop into the building on the driver's side would have required a convoluted series of driveways for ingress and egress. In addition to inviting confusion, such driveways would have meant paving more wooded area than either the staff or the architect felt was worth the effort. The architect's team gave it their best shot, but this was one wonderful idea that just did not work.

Circulation is another workroom that has some storage space, in the form of enough open area to attract anything and everything that does not have a home elsewhere in the library. It has consequently filled up with everything from lost and found boxes to stored copies of a self-published history and miscellaneous unused but beloved leftover furniture from the pre-renovation WL building. As in the reference workroom, banks of flipper door lockers for personal effects are available to staff.

Staff from several departments considered flooring options in the staff work areas. For the hallway and lunchroom, they chose a thick, colorful rubber composite. It is less noisy with carts and shoes than standard vinyl flooring, is easier to clean than carpet, and the color has not noticeably faded even after three and a half years of daily use.

The support services staff had the combined responsibilities of planning their work space at JCCL and preparing a collection for the new facility.

The technical services area at WL was small but efficient, like the steel that surrounds a canned ham. In a space of around 700 square feet was housed a staff of seven and several volunteers; new, mending, and weeded materials; all postal and other deliveries; the Friends of the Library sorting area; the bookmobile staff; and for several years, the library's mainframe computer (back when those were big and noisy). Technical services was understandably consumed with the design of the department's large workroom in the new building. Among their wishes were windows that opened, modular furniture high enough for some privacy between cubicles, and a larger receiving area and mail room. They chose a color scheme from the selections provided by the interior designer, and each person had the flexibility to assign fabrics to flipper doors, chairs, and tackable surfaces as desired in each cubicle.

They realized that their decisions would affect the technical services working environment and those who came after them for a long time. But it was not until they examined the little swatches of fabric, tried out different styles of office chairs and contemplated diagrams of the new work space that the reality of occupying a new library began to take shape. Making these decisions proved harder than many had anticipated because, as with any new project, the desire for quality and quantity had to be balanced with budget restrictions.

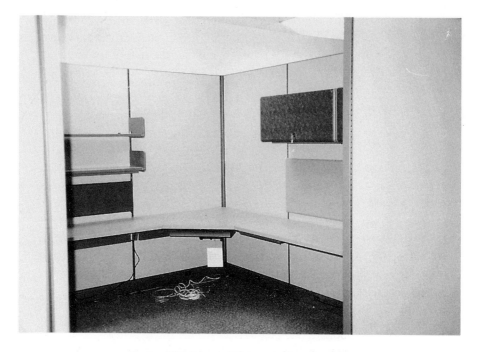

James City County Library staff workstation.

For technical services, choosing the carpet color became the first issue. When staff began discussing carpet, the technical services director imagined that a neutral color like gray or taupe was the way to go. Her director assured her, based on previous experience, that a less neutral color would hold up better and show less dirt. A now-filthy beige carpet at a nearby, year-old public school also convinced staff that maybe the director was right about that. The result is a blue and green shaded carpet pattern that does not appear either color, but rather a soft perception of color. For more than three years the carpet has held up very well, and the staff has decided it's more cheerful to work in a setting of color than one of grays and browns. (Lesson learned: listen to people who've had experience.)

Next they tackled furnishing: end panels, work surfaces, storage units for files, pencil drawers, task lights. The technical services director became intimately familiar with axonometric drawings. Technical services staff tried different desk configurations which vendors supplied for scrutiny, including Paralax units, the glass-topped work surfaces that accommodate computer monitors beneath them. Some staff liked them, others did not. And although some staff chose them for their work areas, few Paralax units that were installed remained in use for more than a year. Our staff did not find them to be effective over a long period of time. (Lesson learned: it's probably best to go with the time-honored solution.) In conjunction with planning for work space, technical services also had to plan for future staff. The expectation that the collections budget would increase with the new library building meant that more staff, and work spaces for them, would be needed to maintain the level of service WRL had heretofore managed. So, workspace expansion beyond accommodating current staff had to be built into the plans.

They decided on private offices for the department head and the acquisitions manager, the latter because the position often works with donors. They chose doors with narrow vertical glass panels for both aesthetic appeal and because it made it easy to see if either person was in or out, or involved in a meeting, although WRL staff with offices generally leave their doors open, so a closed door is usually a clear enough message that the occupant is not to be disturbed.

The catalogers ended up with the window cubicles on the front of the building and the acquisitions and receiving staff got the cubicles on the opposite wall. In the 12 to 15 feet between the cubicle groups, staff planned shelving for new book arrivals, one three-sided cubicle for the processing staff, and another set of shelves for materials waiting to be mended, bound, or reordered. Along another wall of the room they designed a space for carts, a work table for volunteers, and a small three-walled cubicle. Although the center of the room ended up looking somewhat crowded or "busy," it has proved an effective design to provide a measure of privacy straight cubicles do not offer.

Against one wall of technical services is a long counter of standing and sitting height for book processing. There is a sink for washing hands. In retrospect, this area is fairly close to sinks in the staff kitchen and staff restroom and could have been left out, but the book processor at the time thought it was required — maybe we used more glue back then. Installed above the standing height counter are partitioned shelves for storing and organizing different sized book jacket covers flat or on rolls. There is also storage under the counters for labels and other small rolled goods.

Another part of the office space that technical services staff designed was the mail room, because the courier is part of that department. The mail room is connected to the technical services work room by a standard-sized door like the other office doors. A permanent but size-adjustable set of mail slot shelves lines one long wall of the mail room. As with some other features, a set of mail slot shelves this large was something the architect had to be convinced was important. Staff included in the design a wall length counter for mail processing. It was made to accommodate the postage meter, UPS supplies, and working space for the courier. That long counter top is incredibly useful for preparing outgoing mail and sorting the incoming post. Eight free-standing bookshelves for receiving and supply storage (for audio-visual cases, for example) take up about a third of the floor space in the mail room, but storage space always seemed to run short at WL, and shelves were deemed useful in ensuring a smooth mail processing operation. Given an unlimited budget, the mail room is someplace compact shelving might be useful.

Finally, a corner of the mail room is currently the storage area for Friends of the Library books at JCCL. Our only real complaint about the mail room is the gray industrial-grade vinyl flooring that never looks clean, which was installed by the contractor without consulting the library staff or architect. If it had been more than the one room, or discovered earlier in the project, we might have made them take it up, but as it was we left it.

One of the more memorable experiences came when we test-sat patron seating one month. The interior designer arranged for about a dozen vendors to deliver sample chairs for JCCL to the existing library. The project liaison numbered each one and put them in one of the thoroughfare "offices" at WL; in addition to being able to catch all the staff, there just wasn't any other place to put them. Staff and patrons sat in and voted on each chair, with the majority winners getting a second round of test-buns. Fortunately, there are a number of areas in JCCL where we could (and did) use different types of chairs: soft lounge seating in the solarium; more traditional "hard" study seating at tables; and more lounge seating in the young adult area. We even splurged on an expensive rocking chair for parent-child story times in the children's area.

While planning for their future home, technical services staff also planned for the future JCCL collection. Libraries adding a location need to create collections of books, magazines, videos, audio materials, and all the other resources expected in a contemporary library. For WRL this process involved people from all departments at one point or another, but technical services staff oversaw the process. The JCCL opening day collection of 70,000 volumes was half from previously owned library materials and half new purchases. Reference, youth services, and technical services staff handled the former. The technical services department, with help from reference and youth services, enjoyed much of the challenge of developing the purchased collection for JCCL while learning the ins and outs of high volume book purchasing and cataloging.

Opening JCCL offered staff the opportunity to help create a new collection to complement the one housed at WL. Their excitement of having funding for a new collection was tempered by their recognition of the challenge of selecting and ordering approximately 35,000 items for JCCL.

We planned to transfer another 35,000 volumes from WL to JCCL, half of which were donations. All of these donated items were stored in the basement of WL. This storage area, lovingly referred to as "the Pit," held over 13,600 items, mostly books, which had been accumulating there for more than a decade in anticipation of a second building sometime, somewhere. As the reality of JCCL drew closer, this collection became a tangible representation of the new library. The Pit collection had been shelved largely in alphabetical order by author's last name, interfiling fiction and non-fiction together, in the spirit of "if you don't have time today, put it off 'til next year." Fortunately, there weren't too many books whose main entry is the title.

In February 1995, staff began the task of separating the fiction and nonfiction, processing each nonfiction item before reshelving it in call number order. Because of a lack of shelving space we decided that adult biographies would be packed and stored elsewhere. So, while staff separated and reshelved all the other books, they also removed and packed the biographies. By November 1995, staff had reorganized books through the Dewey 700s. With eight months to complete the process there was plenty of time to also select the 19,509 items from the public shelves at WL that would be transferred to JCCL. Reference and youth services staff spent many hours combing through those materials, selecting appropriate items and marking them with hunter green dots.

At roughly the same time that Pit and WL books were being selected and processed, reference and youth services collections librarians were busily selecting new books to add to the opening day collection. One of the first things library management staff had done after the bond referendum passed was solicit bids for the opening day collection. The ideal vendor would be able to deliver all the new books, cassettes, and videos, cataloged and processed perfectly, at a price that satisfied our budgetary restrictions.

From the acquisitions staff's perspective there were specific considerations to be addressed. The acquisitions questions on the RFP were standard: How would the selection lists be created? How current would these selection lists be? How much would the materials cost, including processing and cataloging? What discounts would be offered for materials the vendor had in stock, and what discounts would be offered for the materials that needed to be ordered directly from the publishers? How would "out of print" titles be handled?

Other considerations included how or if the vendor could keep track of the funds spent on adult and juvenile titles in separate accounts. How would the vendor make sure WRL did not make duplicate orders for the same materials, but not restrict the procurement of multiple copies of the same title? At what point could WRL cancel orders already placed? How would the vendor deal with defective or incorrectly processed items or items that were received but had not been ordered?

Processing and cataloging issues were also of prime importance in the RFP. Our youth services collection, as is true of many library collections, consists of books decorated with an amazing array of stickers and dots of various colors and designs. Easy-reader books get Easy Reader stickers on their spines, concept books get blue dots; we have brown dots for number books, pink dots for alphabet books, neon green dots for Mother Goose books. Adult books, too, have different genre labels: mystery, science fiction, short stories, fantasy, and westerns. The spines of 18+ videos have three-quarter inch blue dot stickers that have "18+" typed in the middle, and each video needs a "Be Kind — Rewind!" smiley face sticker on the video itself. We required a vendor who could process these items with all the correct stickers in all the correct places.

Cataloging specifications, of course, required documentation, which we'd provide. We specified that the vendor provide full MARC records and not just incomplete transcriptions of the CIP. Our holdings in OCLC had to be updated correctly and all records had to be easily integrated into our Dynix catalog. One critical consideration was how a vendor would deal with the cataloging of additional copies of items we already had in the WL collection and in Dynix. Thousands of new, duplicate bibliographic records in our system would confuse staff and patrons. And we certainly did not want to pay the vendor for such duplicates to be created. They needed to be integrated into the existing records.

The cataloging peculiarities of any library increase these sorts of complications. We use the first three letters of the main entry for the "cutter" in our non-fiction call numbers, except for books about individual artists or for books about authors, in which case we use the first three letters of the subject. Although we use standard Dewey classification for most non-fiction items, we have different systems for adult, juvenile and young adult fiction, biography, picture books, and easy readers. The classification is not standard for law books, Virginia genealogy, juvenile books on Native Americans, and juvenile geography. Non-feature videos are given call numbers, but feature videos and children's videos are not. Recognizing all these variations, the catalogers wanted online access to the vendor's cataloging database to monitor the cataloging while it was being done. Although they are something we take for granted now, high-speed Internet connections to databases were not commonly available at the time.

Each question fostered another question. Where would the books be stored while the building was being built? How and when would the books be delivered once the building could be occupied? How would the security of these materials before delivery be assured? We specified that the materials needed to be sorted by classification sequence to allow relatively easy shelving once they were delivered. Books ordered from third sources needed to be processed by and stored by the opening-day vendor, and these items, too, needed to be sorted into classification sequences.

Given their responsibility for organizing access to collections, technical services helped to phrase the questions on an RFP for a library materials vendor, and later assisted in choosing the vendor. It took multiple meetings among the technical services manager, the finance director, and the acquisitions manager to complete a list of all the processing and cataloging expectations for the RFP. After the fact, we learned there were still more questions we should have asked.

Baker & Taylor, Ingram, and Brodart submitted bids, which we reviewed carefully, as each vendor had included detailed answers to the questions we had asked. For the acquisitions section each vendor priced the bids somewhat differently, but in the end they were very close to each other. The prices for videos and cassettes came in highest on all of the vendors' proposals. When it came to cataloging, all vendors offered full MARC cataloging for most items, though Baker & Taylor did not offer it (just adaptive or copy cataloging) for items ordered directly from publishers. Two vendors would update the catalog directly via modem and phone line (at WRL's expense). Brodart would create and update the database at their site, but offered WRL a few hours of online access to their database so the cataloging at their end could be checked against our own and vice versa. While the catalogers felt strongly that the vendors who offered direct online access to the newly created database would be best, they understood that other considerations— mainly experience of the vendor, as well as price and availability of materials— were factors just as important as the ability to keep an eye on the quality of the cataloging.

The final selection was made by a committee including the acquisitions manager, the technical services director, the finance director, and the director of the library. Because the prices each vendor offered were so similar, the committee based their decision on the experience the vendors had in projects of this nature. After reviewing the bids, we chose Brodart as the best option.

We decided to go with a set discount rather than a "floating discount" for acquisitions. Once we received the selection lists, however, we realized this may not have been the best choice. Many of our requested items were not available through Brodart. As a result, library staff obtained these themselves through direct orders from the publishers. The vendor, apparently, was unwilling to absorb the cost of doing business with some of the low- or no-discount publishers. The total cost in staff time taken to order and track the many library materials from the various publishers versus the effort to track varying discount rates was difficult to assess, but in retrospect it probably would have been easier to track the varied discount schedule. Also, the higher trade discount probably would have offset the low- or no-discount items.

In their bids, all three vendors were very ambiguous about the types of discounts they offered. When the process of ordering was underway, we began to understand why. The bids said, in effect, "Books from small presses, etc., may be discounted at a lesser rate from 0 to '$x$' discount based on the discount the vendor receives." This 0 to "$x$" discount is a very gray area. We found there was no in-between discount or a very small discount given to the library when in some cases the vendor received a substantial discount on the items. Perhaps the RFP should have explored more thoroughly areas such as how much the vendor would discount an item if the discount they receive from the publisher was 40 percent versus 55 percent. Some vendors always discount trade titles from major publishers no matter when the books were published; other vendors consider older, single-copy trade orders as short discounts. We also learned that choosing a vendor who can deal directly with some of the large reference publishers is important, since being able to place the orders with one source can translate to cost savings for the library.

In terms of paying for the new items, our situation may not have been unique, but it was a big change for WRL, an independent agency used to doing its own purchasing. Because the JCCL project was funded by a bond referendum, all of our bills had to be sent to the county government for payment. It certainly was a learning experience for the county — they had never paid invoices for books and library materials before. After a somewhat rocky start, including a long lag time between receipt of invoices and payment, we worked with county staff to devise a system for forwarding the bills and invoice questions to the correct county departments.

No library materials were ordered through the acquisitions module of our library database, which made tracking difficult in budgeting and ongoing ordering procedures. If we had it to do over again (heaven help us), we would create a dummy budget in our database and track the materials as they were invoiced. This would have been much easier than following the convoluted paper trails.

After WRL selected Brodart, a cataloger from that company visited to learn our procedures for processing materials. The representative asked us to prepare specifications for how each type of item was processed. The individual steps were broken down, examined and written out. Colorful pages with dots and stickers emerged from the project. To our benefit, this exercise allowed for the concurrent production of an accurate procedures manual for our own use with detailed processing instructions for each collection in the library displayed in a clear, easy-to-read format.

The automated services department worked with our catalog vendor to create an OMR (Output MARC Records) program and an LMR (Load MARC Records) program so we could share a copy of our database with Brodart and later load the new MARC records they had created into our catalog. Brodart agreed to attach 949 fields listing a barcode to the bibliographic records for each new holding we ordered. For new copies of an item that already had a bibliographic record, Brodart used the pre-existing record in our database and only attached a 949 field for each added holding. When we loaded the new and updated MARC records into our database, the LMR program used the bib number as a match point, overlaying the old record on the new. We asked Brodart not to send back unchanged records for which we did not order additional copies; during this year long process, we knew we would delete items from Dynix and we did not want these records to be added back into the system.

When we sent samples of the cataloging and processing to Brodart, we could see where we needed to clarify instructions. It took daily, then weekly phone calls, between the technical services director and the cataloger at Brodart in charge of our collection to reach an acceptable level of understanding.

A full year prior to the anticipated opening of JCCL, the reference department began its part in the process of selecting adult materials for the new building from titles already held at WL. At WRL, each reference librarian is responsible for a designated part of the collection, and so each combed the appropriate shelves in quest of likely items. Armed with green dot stickers (to be placed on the books' back covers) and Telxons (portable inventory devices that read barcodes), the librarians identified books selected for JCCL physically and electronically. The green-dotted items remained in the stacks and circulated as usual. The librarians also descended to the Pit and decided which of the duplicate and inactive books should be retained for the new collection. The additional processing required for these materials was carried out by the technical services department, as described earlier in the chapter. When not green-dotting or Pit–visiting, the reference librarians completed their collection profiles for the opening day collection for Brodart. Included in the profiles were the titles already owned and the review sources to be used by the vendor in assembling customized selection lists.

In response to the librarians' collection specifications, the vendor promptly sent six large boxes of printouts. To their dismay, the librarians discovered that the selection lists were not printed in any discernible order, so they embarked on the tedious task of separating adult and children's titles, imposing Dewey call number arrangement, eliminating duplicate pages, and deciphering publisher and reviewer source codes. This accomplished, the lists presented additional challenges. Title matches were actually ISBN matches, thus amounting to suggestions for the purchase of titles already owned in other editions. Ultimately, the lists did not provide a sufficient number of desirable materials. Nevertheless, the librarians made selections and returned their annotated lists to the vendor. Three months passed and a second set of lists arrived: many selected titles had proved to be unavailable, so there was lots of opening day collection budget left to spend. Within two weeks, librarians completed another order and, as a corrective measure, included photocopied pages from four months of review journals to request titles perpetually absent from the vendor lists. The ordered materials would not be displayed in the library's online catalog until the arrival of the entire database and the books themselves about a month before the opening of JCCL.

During the month prior to opening day, staff members from all departments pulled and boxed all the green-dotted items on the shelves. Automated services decided on a method for preventing the materials from appearing on the public electronic catalog, using the New Building agency. Although up to this point the items were physically available, we left the JCCL books in a separate agency so when we did pull them and pack them we didn't need to scan their barcodes again. Books that had escaped packing and were returned by patrons in subsequent months were simply transferred to the new building as they were checked in at WL. The reference staff routinely had added duplicate copies of current fiction to the stored collection for some time, and when books from the Pit joined the green-dots and Brodarts at JCCL, complete hardback runs of popular authors appeared on the shelves. Similarly, duplicate periodical subscriptions had been established earlier in the year and stored until the new building opened, so JCCL had at least six months of back issues of popular magazines on opening day in July 1996. The three components of the new collection, plus intermittent receipts of direct orders, were combined and shelved by collection services staff. Opening a new building allowed librarians to plan and institute new shelving arrangements. In a departure from shelving schemes at WL, adult mystery, science fiction and short story titles were interfiled with general fiction titles. Documentaries and other non-fiction videos were shelved with books in the appropriate call number. This arrangement helped to maximize space, speed up shelving, and alert patrons to more than one genre by a single author or materials format about a single topic.

That is not to say that patrons were universally happy about the interfiling schemes—a few mystery fans in particular did not appreciate the idea of sorting through the chaff of other fiction to get to their favorites. Reference staff took individual concerns one at a time and introduced patrons to what we saw as the advantages of shelving all types of fiction together. Some of the concerns were abated when readers found other non-mysteries by their favorite authors, and all of them appreciated the individual attention.

# 3

# Renovating Old

Before the last book was shelved and the last PC was unpacked at JCCL, work began on the renovation of the Williamsburg Library building. The WL renovation was accomplished in phases so the building could remain open to the public during construction. Each stage presented special challenges for personnel, indeed for whole departments in the building. With the experiences of JCCL construction vivid in our minds, we approached this new construction project feeling more confident, but also less naive. JCCL is a beautiful library, but as we have related, not everything went as we had planned. As it turned out, the library's project liaison (different from JCCL's liaison) and director had to follow the WL architect and contractors much more closely than we did at JCCL, and the WL architect was not as receptive to staff suggestions. Fresh from the JCCL project, staff took perhaps greater interest in the WL project because of our JCCL missteps and because staff and patrons were in the building during the work. Construction is difficult to ignore when power tools and earth-moving machinery are introduced to the library service environment.

WL's renovation was planned in three phases. The library director explained at the time, "Although this scenario falls short of offering optimum service to our patrons during the construction period, I believe that we can offer better service through a phased approach than if the entire building were closed during the construction period and we tried to offer service through alternative means." Even though the new JCCL was open and completely functional, WL serves pedestrians and neighborhood patrons who would probably go without library service rather than travel nine miles to visit JCCL.

To imagine the renovation, picture a mime whose box is expanding as he pushes out. The building's footprint had very little room to expand, so the architect added a few feet on each side of the building to make it work. A complication not all library systems will encounter (we hope) is a local Architectural Review Board (ARB). WL is located in an historic area, so every building's plans (even just a paint change) have to be approved by the ARB. WL's first phase had youth services and the former adult area open while the new adult addition was constructed. Then adult services moved into the new part of the building while the old adult area was renovated. And last, youth services closed for renovations, with the new and renovated adult areas opened.

Since the first construction phase involved demolition in the former administrative area, for much of the time all the administrative offices were moved to the part of the building where technical services had been located (the entire technical services operation was moved to JCCL a few weeks after the grand opening). Crowded into one space were the offices of the library director and human resources director, with work space for collection services, circulation, and reference. The space was quickly dubbed TAFKATS, The Area Formerly Known As Tech Services.

With the expansion of the reference staff during the months immediately preceding the opening of the James City County Library, "off-desk" work space in the Williamsburg building became constricted. "The Nook," a narrow space about six by 12 feet, was packed with filing cabinets, shelves,

Earth-moving equipment at Williamsburg Library, April 1997.

review journals, software manuals, and a large plastic wastebasket poised beneath a makeshift drain to catch water from leaks originating on the roof. In this space about a dozen reference librarians, several assistants and clerks, and a few volunteers shared three computers and attempted to carry out collection development, outreach, and planning projects when they weren't working the desk. Even after the new building opened and the staff split into two teams that rotated between buildings, the space remained cramped. All departments scheduled as many off-desk hours at JCCL as possible during construction at WL, but staff still needed a little off-desk work space at WL. As the renovation of the Williamsburg building progressed and staff was displaced from the Nook, one departmental space-planner devised a temporary office labeled "the Alcove," which was used briefly until the new addition became available. Though about half the size of the Nook, it nevertheless provided a reasonably private work space, complete with a computer and some storage. Perseverance, patience, and humor were requirements for staff.

When the renovated section of the building was granted an occupancy permit, library staff from all departments pitched in to retrieve stored books and shift other parts of the collection. Decisions made during the planning phase guided the process; as at JCCL, reference librarians seized the opportunity to interfile mysteries, science fiction, short stories, and general fiction. Genre labels had been applied prior to the construction period in anticipation of the new shelving system. Staff also decided to eliminate hanging files in the adult stacks, so language cassettes were repackaged, reclassified with Dewey numbers, and placed on the circulating shelves. More abundant shelf space in the new reference stacks also inspired the translation of many years' worth of vertical pamphlet files into fully cataloged "reference notebooks." Rational planning, however, sometimes collides with irrational developments (reminder: Expect the unexpected). The portage of circulating Dewey 900s from the second to the first floor awaited completion of the new public elevator. On the appointed day, reference staff had barely started to shift the books when the elevator ceased functioning. Like a bucket brigade, reference staff called on skills they'd honed moving the reference collection during another phase of construction. They formed teams and relayed the 900s down the stairway, onto carts and the waiting shelves. Dropping books from the second floor balcony was another option, but it would have been awkward to preserve the Dewey order that way.

Reference staff (and the rest of the library) learned a good amount about shifting a collection as a result of the three phases of construction. Before they were done they knew how to calculate linear feet and average

**Williamsburg Regional Library staff unpack stored books.**

height of books when planning shelving, and to make sure what the contractor delivered matched the specifications. In terms of moving books, they found that teams of two worked well — one to remove or replace books, one to load or unload a cart — plus someone to make sure the teams didn't get a cart out of order. Librarians traded tasks periodically for a little variety and to avoid overworking a single set of muscles. Related to that was working with small handfuls of books rather than all that a person could hold. Big loads may seem to move more books faster, but they also contribute to fatigue and burnout. The last lesson was to assess the final shelving arrangement functionally and aesthetically.

As you might imagine, it was easy for a department to become engrossed in what affected them. A support mechanism that helped staff handle the vagaries of construction was a series of regular updates on construction progress. E-mails to all staff kept people informed by explaining what was happening, what noises were expected, and answering questions that one staff member might voice, but probably were unspoken by dozens. While e-mail had been a regular part of our workdays for at least ten years, during construction and renovation it became a critical communications tool for reaching everyone on staff, potentially at the same time (depending on when people opened their e-mail). The practice of weekly and sometimes daily e-mail updates started from the very beginning of the renovation project. The contractor was chosen during the last days of October 1996. A week later our library director sent e-mail that set the tone for the entire project. She wrote, "During this most odd time of trying to provide service in a building that is under construction, and whose parking, already limited, becomes even worse, departments are welcome to experiment with any sort of schedule that doesn't affect public service. This could certainly include more work being done at home, and even four-day work-weeks. Could be that having to be even more flexible and creative during the coming months will generate long-term benefits in all sorts of areas, not just that at the end of this we'll have a wonderful new-ish building and more parking and a beautiful greenspace actually named The Library Plaza. Sends chills up my spine just thinking about it. Thanks in advance for all of that creativity and flexibility." With that we were off on a dizzying if sometimes frustrating adventure.

Despite our best efforts, a variety of construction details proved beyond our ability to direct. At JCCL we were able to concentrate on the building and that was it. At WL we were trying to conduct regular library business and follow construction progress at the same time. When the contractor or the project liaison had a question, we had to shift on the fly from thinking about running a library to thinking about building one. As a result, after grinding our gears more than once, we relied more heavily on the judgment of the library's project liaison (who was very reliable) because there just was not time to seek group opinions. Staff who had been more involved with the JCCL project sometimes bristled at what they perceived to be purposeful exclusion, but with renovations continuing apace, there was rarely time to smooth feathers.

Again, each department had distinct experiences that affected and reflected the renovation process. For youth services there were examples of communication misunderstandings and occasional detail omissions. There was also incredible innovation and creativity that resulted from the renovation.

Once again youth services designated large areas to be finished as tackable surface. This architect abided by our wishes and we got all the tackable walls we wanted. However, instead of using standard cork board or a similar material, the architect inserted a fabric covered material called whisper board. While it is attractive, we discovered that it has some significant drawbacks.

At the last minute, we learned a crucial piece of information about the Whisper Board. Special aluminum push pins with extra long shafts are required for tacking things into it. The malevolent-looking push pins are very expensive (around $10 per hundred), but left with no alternatives, we ordered about a thousand of them. After starting to use them, our concern became how long they would remain in the walls. Things like push pins regularly get "borrowed" from the children's departments, but at least they don't look like everyone else's pins.

To our surprise, we learned that the primary reason the specialized pins don't remain in the walls is that the Whisper Board is so soft. This is particularly true when using big pieces of background paper for displays. We can tack up anything we want in the WL children's area. We just have to be willing to keep re-tacking and be vigilant in retrieving the push pins from the floor so that the small patrons and their adult companions don't poke themselves.

While youth services had to contend with tackable surfaces, automated services faced different technical challenges with the renovation. Perhaps the most pressing one was keeping electronic services like circulation's check-out computers up and running while the building was being torn down and reconstructed around us.

The first stage of construction meant the addition of a new wing and a redesign of existing office spaces at WL. With everything shifting, check-in and check-out areas had to be relocated, along with all administrative, circulation and reference offices. The check-out desk came to share space with the program services desk in the library's theatre lobby. While this was a good cross-training opportunity for both departments, it meant that a network signal had to be maintained for three check-out stations, two catalog terminals, and the meeting room reservation station that already existed in that location, all from a single network cable which serviced the space. By setting up a mini–LAN using a terminal server and hub, it was possible to get the signal to all the computers. But there were daily unpredictable battles to keep these tenuous connections alive and healthy for 18 months of cramped, intensive use and various construction stresses.

The most significant challenge circulation staff faced during the WL project was remaining cheerful in the midst of construction and trying to respond to patron questions about the renovation in a positive way. For much of the time inadequate parking was the biggest complaint from patrons because much of the already scarce parking was usurped by construction equipment and construction of the actual expanded building. With the floor plan changing every few months for almost a year and half, circulation staff had to constantly revise the directions they gave patrons on how to get to a specific part of the library on any given day. Circulation office space was very small. In TAFKATS, circulation had enough room at one of the cataloger's former work stations to answer the telephone, print out morning reports, and store handbags. We soon began printing all the reports we could at JCCL: besides the advantages of reducing numbers of staff at WL and abbreviating the noise of a dot-matrix printer in TAFKATS, the mail room was at JCCL and notices would be sent to patrons from there. Shelf checks were nearly useless during the renovation, so protests of claimed returns from patrons were difficult to disprove. As soon as it was mechanically possible, we began forwarding incoming telephone calls to JCCL as well.

Taking lessons learned from building JCCL, automated services followed the pattern already established for planning for location and amount of cable, numbers and types of connections, equipment, and software. For future flexibility, we again chose to terminate cable connections at the wall rather than in modular office wall panels. Category 5 cable was once again used only for network connections. Using each department's analysis of its workflow, automated services drafted lists of required equipment and software. A complete inventory of existing equipment was compiled to determine what could continue to be used and what needed to be replaced. An equipment budget was not part of the renovation budget, so we looked at other places in the budget that might have a flexible margin. As we'll discuss in a later chapter, we ended up designing and bidding out our own furniture specifications. This, plus a generous grant from the Clark Foundation, plus a windfall modular furniture donation, allowed us to carve out almost $15,000 for computers and peripheral equipment. Six months prior to the expected completion of the first phase of construction, a list of equipment and software needs was ready for the library's purchasing agent to prepare bid packets. With this lead time, purchases for all construction phases could be bid together with delivery times specified, netting greater savings. Delivery and installation of equipment was satisfactorily completed by opening day.

At WRL, program services is a separate department whose staff manages meeting room set ups and reservations and plans and promotes library-sponsored adult programs (we know — we're blessed). The department includes a director, a full-time technician, a graphics manager, and two additional part-time technicians, all of whom work closely with patrons, Friends, and library personnel to execute detailed logistical arrangements related to use of the library's meeting spaces. They are very much on the front lines and had to deal not only with the constraints on meeting room accessibility created by construction, but also with as many patron questions as the other public service desks. In addition, with experience in promoting programs, they became responsible for making sure that the public was kept informed through news releases, announcements, flyers, word of mouth, etc.

Part of the furniture purchased with a grant from the Clark foundation.

Prior to the renovation, program services had operated two meeting rooms at WL — one with a 60-person capacity and the other accommodating 24 people — and a 266–seat theatre. As part of the renovation, the larger meeting room became office space, while a new meeting room with a window and a capacity of about 45 was created from what was once a staff copier room and office space. The 24-person meeting room remained and a new 20 person meeting room was also converted from former office space. The library's theatre was not renovated, but construction affected it nonetheless. The WL theatre has become a central venue for community performing arts groups and library-sponsored concerts of folk and jazz music throughout the year. WRL's own concert series traditionally is well attended, attracting almost 4,000 people per season. Attendance dropped when renovations began.

However, both patron and library use of the meeting rooms and theatre remained heavy. Between July 1996 and June 1997 more than 12,000 patrons used these rooms for their own meetings or programs. Another 33,000 people attended adult and children's library programs held in the rooms or the theatre. Groups using the library's meeting facilities included a cross-section of the community's cultural, social, and religious organizations. City and county government officials used the library for public and departmental meetings. Two performing arts groups, the Williamsburg Chamber Music Association and the Tidewater Classical Guitar Society, performed exclusively in the library theatre for their Williamsburg concerts. Several area dance groups reserved the theatre to hold periodic recitals and the meeting rooms served as overflow dressing spaces.

The disruption of these facilities during the planned 18 months of renovation at WL was expected to generate a significant burden not only for the community, but also for library programming. When the scope of the construction process became known, program services staff realized they had to initiate three approaches to minimize patron inconvenience: inform patrons of impending disruptions; coordinate with construction crews to minimize the disruptive impact; and, as a last resort, reschedule uses to other facilities or around construction conflicts.

Of primary concern was the patrons' need to know. While staff might receive weekly e-mail updates by virtue of working in the library, patrons did not. The general public was informed of construction plans and closings through regular publicity channels that most libraries are already using for their programs and services. For us, these included newspaper articles, public service announcements to radio and TV stations, flyers or posters distributed around the building and community, and the monthly library newsletter, funded by the Friends. In terms of meeting room and theatre reservations, program services staff proactively worked to minimize inconveniences. They categorized users into two groups: those using meeting rooms on a regular basis and those who were "itinerant" users.

The regular users included library departments and library-sponsored organizations, as well as community organizations. WRL does not charge a fee for meeting room space if a nonprofit group holds a meeting no more than once a month. We had scores of diverse groups who fell into this category. More frequently scheduled organizations included a storytelling organization, a photography club, a group of poets who meet weekly, and the local Internet users association. Before construction began, many of these groups were notified by letter of some of the "planned" key disruptions—phased closure of the building, tearing up of the parking lot, etc. This was especially critical for some of the performing arts groups to know, as they booked performers up to a year in advance.

Our "itinerant" or casual meeting room users include those organizations that meet at the library periodically, but not on a regular basis. They could generally be told of "planned" disruptions at the time they registered for the room use, but there were exceptions. One group – a health care provider—wanted to conduct a mini-medical school in our theatre over a six week period. They expected up to 250 people to attend each session. This group fit into the itinerant category, but because of their extended and heavy use of the theatre, staff worked closely with them to ensure there was no conflict between what they needed and the expected disruptions caused by construction work.

In reality, most anticipated timetables of specific projects or disruptions did not coincide with the actual construction. It sounds obvious to us now, but when starting a renovation project library staff and library patrons must be prepared for this type of scheduling uncertainty. Despite agreed-upon start dates and end dates, things will change. You can guess and hope when something will happen, but unforeseeable factors like delays in the arrival or condition of construction materials, the weather, design changes, and other project delays are likely to throw numerous proverbial wrenches into the works.

Even when we grew to understand that delays should be expected, the disruptions did not become easier to handle. We had patrons sign a statement acknowledging that they understood that they were using the facility during a time of disruptions and that WRL could not be held entirely responsible for construction related problems during any program. This agreement was fairly informal, although a more binding waiver probably would have been appropriate. The mini-medical school, for example, had to put up with a couple of weeks when there was no carpeting on the floor as they came into the building. Their preference for a large meeting space in a neutral public setting like the library made up for this inconvenience, fortunately.

Advising patrons of upcoming disruptions had at least one unintended benefit for the library. Parking issues were a side battle associated with the construction at WL. A plan to truncate the library parking during the renovation process was modified due, in part, to the lobbying efforts of one of the performing arts groups who used the theatre for their concerts. They complained to city officials and their voices seemed to carry more weight than did the library's. We have found, as most libraries do, that citizen action can be a powerful motivator for convincing elected officials of library needs.

Knowing ahead of time about severe disruptions that would adversely affect the potential use of the meeting spaces gave program services staff opportunity to reschedule groups that were going to use the spaces during those periods of uncertainty. Although we initially understood that there would be little impact on the meeting rooms, program services staff soon realized that toward the end of the renovation that the entire theatre wing of the library (which also includes youth services) would be effectively shut down. Knowing that in plenty of time gave us the chance to work with patrons to find alternative spaces for their meetings. One option that materialized was the city council meeting room, across the street from WL. That worked for several groups whose gatherings were held at times when council was not in its chambers.

WRL was also fortunate, in many respects, to have the James City County Library already completed. Some rescheduling was simply a matter of moving programs to that building. That did not always work, since some organizations had chosen a particular building for a very specific reason, such as convenience for their members. In our community we had to accept the fact that patrons accustomed to using WL, in the heart of the historic city, considered JCCL to be remote ("halfway to Richmond" became a favorite quotation). They would not travel to the other building because the 15 minutes' distance was unappealing or they did not know where it was. (We have offered maps showing routes between WL and JCCL since the latter opened, but some devoted WL users still avoid JCCL. Happily, once patrons discover JCCL, they often become regulars at both buildings.)

These examples led to the one result of the construction that did not affect patrons as such, but did affect the library. There was some increase in meeting room usage at JCCL, but the relative newness of that facility combined with the perception of its distance to prevent the use of JCCL meeting space from substantially climbing. Perhaps surprisingly, our over-all usage did not fall during the renovation. The combined building totals for circulation, reference questions, electronic services, meeting room use, and program attendance actually climbed.

Program services received frequent updates on the construction plan from the hired project manager in order to try to keep library events from intersecting with construction events. The staff learned an important lesson early that the construction plan is just a guideline; it is not carved in stone. Problems and conflicts can and will disrupt the plan. The program services director gave the project manager key program dates on a regular basis telling him things like, "OK, you can't cut off the plumbing this day because we have a big program with lots of people expected." Being direct helped get the point across. Perhaps the most useful thing our program services director did was to establish good relations with the construction supervisors and key personnel. That paid off when it came to the crunch times when things do not go according to plan. It also helped the construction people understand what WRL priorities were. Again, to library staff this sounds obvious, but the priority of the construction people is getting the job done and making a profit for their company. They do not consider keeping the noise down so as not to disturb the community college class a high priority. Being able to assert and discuss the concerns of WRL with them went a long way toward helping to establish mutually agreeable priorities. At least it kept a stressful situation from turning into a shouting match. (Or after the occasional shouting match, it made the reconciliation less of a problem.) We still ended up with a disturbed community college class, but at least we were able to tell the students in advance that there would be noise. And on days with nice weather it gave the class an excuse to move outside. The main lesson taken by the program services director was that the more informed you can be, and the more you can inform others — patrons, staff and construction people — the better.

There were many aspects of the renovation project that program services (and for that matter the rest of the staff) could not anticipate. They did not expect the noise level to be as high as it was, even when work was going on in different parts of the building. That created some real problems for the community college class held in WL meeting rooms on a regular basis. The jackhammering that was going on 100 feet away from the rooms carried through the walls and the ceiling, making it nearly impossible for students to concentrate on their studies. They eventually had to relocate their work to another building in town.

Temperature fluctuations were also challenging. When a new heating and air conditioning system was installed the program services end of the building was without heat for several weeks during the middle of winter. For some of that time there was no airflow at all. That made it difficult for patrons and staff. Difficulties arose also when utilities were interrupted. With a project the size of the WL renovation, at various times we lost electricity, plumbing, electronic networks, and telephone service. We had to figure out ahead of time how to provide service to patrons and staff when one of these utilities was cut. We learned to direct patrons to alternate restrooms, to explain why the library was too cold or too hot, as well as be prepared ourselves to not be able to make or receive phone calls or to lose access to our computer systems. Luckily, we rarely had everything out of commission at the same time.

One of the most difficult lessons to accept was learned first-hand by the program services director, because of the relationships he maintained with construction coordinators and others connected to the renovation project. That lesson was that he (and all of us) had to scrutinize the work being done. Construction is like any business— it exists to make money. Sometimes the way money is made is by cutting corners and telling people that projects are done right, or will be done right, when they are not going to be completed properly at all. Any library staff who had any responsibility for a specific part of the construction project had to be very careful to follow up when told that something was done. "The devil is in the details" became our mantra.

This disappointment did not just apply to dealings with out-of-town construction crews, but sometimes with people in the community, including, as youth services found out, architects who were supposed to be working for (or at least with) us. If a city official promises something will be included as part of the construction project — for example, new meeting room chairs will be purchased — make sure that the something is specified in writing. For a person who is good to his or her own word it can be a shock to find out that not everyone is scrupulously honest. Likewise, for a staff that goes above and beyond to find a complete and accurate (that is, the best) answer to each patron's question, the importance of invoking a healthy skepticism in dealing with some of the construction professionals was a sad lesson to learn.

On a happier note, some of the construction professionals went out of their way to do things better than necessary. As we mention, electricians donated their time to hook up the temporary air conditioner. And even though youth services was scheduled to be closed for six months, the workers completed that phase in three months. The library's liaison became adept at communicating with the construction manager and the subcontractor crews. She learned to read the plans and do research ahead of scheduled work, so she could more easily determine and question what was happening. She was in the field from dawn to dusk most days, because construction crews usually start early. Especially for an occupied building project like WL, getting projects done before we opened was beneficial.

Beyond ensuring we got the building we expected, there were distinct advantages to keeping fully abreast of each step and each individual piece of the renovation project. It also saved us on construction costs. Astute WRL staff recycled old parts from WL and items left over from the assembly of JCCL and used them during the renovation project.

Before rooms were demolished we salvaged whatever materials we could from them. The remodeled kitchen in the basement received solid wood cabinet work from the old graphics room, which was slated to be demolished and new cabinets installed. By reusing the existing cabinets, which were practically new themselves, we saved money that we were able to put toward things that needed replacing. Some outlet covers were reused. Ceiling tiles in some areas were kept, although the bulk was replaced because of the new tile grid system that was installed to accommodate the sprinkler system. Anywhere we could reuse, we did.

Automated services staff managed to save the library several thousand dollars by tracking spare parts available from the JCCL construction project. Surplus materials included 63 cables, 12 foot and 18 foot, left behind by the installer. To our surprise, we could also reuse 100 station cables at WL left over from installations before the renovation. These savings were combined with money saved when one of the staff recommended buying additional cables direct from distributors rather than settling for the marked up price offered by the cabling installation company.

Attention to details continued to pay off because automated services knew how many connections and what equipment went in which rooms. Our staff checked installation work by subcontractors putting cables in and made sure we could hook up what we wanted to hook up. We also critically assessed the cabling company's proposal and concluded that we could live without all 270 cables, since there would only be 132 active data ports at opening and not all of them would have equipment on them. Time will tell what this cost us in flexibility, but the dollar savings was apparent immediately.

Automated services saved more than $3,000 outright just using surplus equipment. The direct purchase of 80,000 feet of category 5 cable realized a savings of more than 50 percent (cost was $11,000 rather than the near $25,000 quoted us by the contractor). Including the direct purchase by library staff of port boards ($5,014), color patch cables ($1,171), and our own purchase of bulk cable ($13,000), total savings reached over

**Patrons use the renovated Williamsburg Library (photograph by David Scherer).**

$22,500. In a budget of over $3 million this sounds insignificant. However, by this time in the project we had reached an impasse with the architect and were designing our own interiors; so every little savings added up.

Another large cost savings arose as a matter of good timing and the generosity of the City of Williamsburg. We mentioned earlier that the WL renovation was part of a larger city endeavor that included a school, parking facility, and plaza. The city liaison for all these projects was also involved with the library renovation. While renovations were occurring at WL, an office building purchased by the city was being prepared for demolition. The previous owners of the building left modular furniture with the building, and the city gave it to the library. All we had to do was disassemble it, move it, and reassemble it. We were able to furnish almost all of the staff office spaces in WL using this furniture, which looked as good as new to us. That was a tremendous cost savings we had not expected. The building was right across the street from the library, so we didn't have to pay any hauling costs. Clearly, this occurrence was more luck than skill, but never underestimate the potential of luck.

The rededication of WL was scheduled for April 26, 1998. On April 20 the library was a swarm of activity. Workmen running cables, installing telephone equipment, adding modular furniture, and putting the final touches on the building roamed around the library from early morning to late night. At the end of a construction project the chaotic environment suddenly changes into a new building and everything that must be ready for opening day is ready.

The renovated library is wonderful in a very different way from JCCL. It is cozier because of lower ceilings, more interior walls, and fewer windows. We have quite a bit of closet space, in addition to the original basement storage area. While JCCL is light, WL is elegant and warm. The Williamsburg Library renovation project was in many ways more stressful for more people than building JCCL. But we believe keeping the building open and phasing the construction served our patrons more effectively than closing the building, and we don't regret it. In spite of the many frustrations of providing library service in a construction zone, the patience and appreciation regularly shown by our patrons made it all worthwhile.

# SECTION II

*Building*

# 4

# Patron and Staff Considerations

The construction of the James City County Library had no direct effect on library patrons or most staff. The hammering, drilling, sawing, welding, roofing, and other construction related noises were on a construction site that even the staff most directly involved visited no more than once a week. Visiting that construction site was an adventure. But the renovation of the Williamsburg Library was an entirely different story. The inconveniences, discomforts, and questions that occur while trying to do work in the library while construction is being done run the gamut. They include lack of climate control, loud noises, closed sections of the library, foul smells, migrating collections, cramped working conditions, dirt, phone problems, power outages, patrons who didn't expect the construction, patrons who knew how to do it better than we did, and unhappy staff. What kept us going were the loyal, cheerful, often elderly patrons who kept coming to the library, checking out books, and telling us how wonderful it would all be when it was done; and the children who, despite their parents' complaints, thought all the construction equipment was really cool.

With a renovation, the inconveniences start immediately and get worse before they get better. Groundbreaking for the expansion of the WL was in December 1996. By February 1997 patrons and staff were starting to feel the renovation blues, as steel girders came together outside for the addition and the first of a series of temporary walls was constructed inside the building. As soon as construction began there were concerns about keeping our inquisitive younger patrons out of harm's way. It was imperative that doors to construction areas remained locked, especially once the summer reading program began.

We fielded complaints from patrons about all sorts of things, including the cutting of a large, beautiful Japanese maple tree rumored to be a

*Top and bottom:* Exterior and interior of James City County Library under construction.

*Left to right:* Channing Hall, Chips Houghland, Linda Massie, Patsy Hansel, Ursula Murden and Ken Wolfe break ground while Gil Granger looks on.

gift to the library years ago (it had to be removed because that's where the children's wing was expanding). During several weeks the book drops were in and out of service, sometimes accessible, oft times blocked. Further confusing patrons was that inside book drop locations became peripatetic as the locus of construction continually changed. Disappearing book drops had more than one patron upset with us.

Then there was the repeated rerouting of foot traffic. With a phased approach this is difficult to avoid. When the old adult area was closed, patrons had access to the new area through a meeting room (did we mention the disruption of meeting room space?). At various stages some entrances to the building were open while others were closed and sometimes papered over from the inside. There was even a time when people could not walk through the building to go from the new reference section to the old youth services wing. They had to leave the building and walk around. At one point, administration staff took turns sitting by the entrance and offering directions to patrons before they got too far. Just as anyone learned a new route, of course, construction dictated a change.

It was hard to keep certain services available to the public. We lost one of our public photocopiers in February. It had to go because of construction constraints (space, dirt, water, etc.). Soon afterwards our ancient public water fountain gave out. Rather than replace it immediately we decided that waiting until the completion of the project made more sense. Why introduce a new piece of equipment into an environment that would age it quickly? We probably would have had to remove a new one later in the construction process anyway. Patrons accustomed to being able to drink from the water fountain were provided with paper cups that could be filled in the nearby restrooms. Not an ideal solution, but people adapted. In retrospect the renovation probably would have been a great time to introduce soda machines.

In May new problems arose when Tidewater Virginia temperatures began to rise and the library's air conditioning unit ground to a halt. The renovations included new air conditioning equipment, but that would not be installed for at least six months. In response to the loss of air conditioning, the library director sent an e-mail message to all staff on handling irritated patrons. There was no good way to soothe patrons except to say that we were trying to "offer great library service in the middle of a construction zone." We hoped for and relied on continued patience and good humor through everything. In an attempt to relieve desk staff from repeated questions about the heat, we posted large signs explaining the situation and apologizing for the unusually warm temperatures in the building.

Anyone who has experienced southeastern Virginia in June knows that an un-air conditioned building can be very uncomfortable. The first step toward battling the heat was to allow staff to dress for comfort. There was no reason staff had to wear businesslike clothing in an 85 degree building. The next step was to develop a procedure for handling the heat, titled Extreme Temperature Operating Procedure, or ETOP for short. ETOP kicked in when the temperature in any part of the library reached 90 degrees. (Just to show that creativity can't be smothered, staff challenged each other to find the hottest place to put the thermometer.) If ETOP was declared, all non-essential staff retreated to JCCL. Staff volunteering to stay behind received time and a half compensation. We displayed signs at all public entrances warning patrons of the extreme heat and that only minimal service would be available in the library. ETOP was only invoked a few times, because in July we found a solution to the temperature problems. It had become obvious very quickly that we would be under ETOP (or mutiny) most of the summer if a temporary fix wasn't found.

Initially we added air conditioning units in windows and installed some in the temporary wall. But even with fans blowing the cool air into and around the building, this was not nearly enough to cool an entire building. The most effective solution was affectionately known as the great bubble machine. The bubble machine was actually a giant temporary air conditioning unit. It snaked through WL with a three foot diameter flexible, plastic tube with holes in the sides attached to the ceiling — like the ultimate drip hose, but for cool air instead of water. The company doing all the electrical connections for the renovations donated their time to complete the electrical hookup for the bubble machine. (No doubt that was enlightened self interest, since they had to work inside too, but we gratefully accepted the charity.)

The bubble machine brought temperatures down to a bearable level. Anyone who really wanted to cool off could go upstairs and stand directly in front of the air flow from the tube, where most patrons had to duck to avoid walking into the flexible hose.

As we all know, whatever Murphy's solution, other problems will be created by it. The temporary air conditioning unit came with its own troubles. One was the price tag — $14,000 for the four months we used it. That meant $14,000 we would not have later, but given wear and tear on library materials, machines, and people, it was a price we had to pay. There were complaints from the library's neighbors. People living across the street complained that the house-sized compressor turned on at 3 a.m. and woke them up. They were right. When the internal thermostat climbed to its unoccupied temperature setting, the compressor kicked on. We set the thermostat up higher, but on hot nights the compressor still came on. If

Temporary air conditioner, also known as the great bubble machine.

we set it too high, we would be unable to cool the library down the next morning. The lesson we learned here was to be prepared to apologize often and sincerely. Many details of the construction project were beyond our control. Generally we found it best to apologize for the inconvenience and try to explain — briefly — why the problem exists.

The temporary bubble machine did not solve our comfort problems entirely; quite a few times during the renovation process we experienced periods of heat without air conditioning. In February 1998 we faced a few weeks of increased temperatures, during one of Virginia's freak and normally welcome warm spells. With the bubble machine long gone and the new air handlers not fully enabled, temperatures in the older part of the building rose. This was especially a problem in the library theatre, where the air was almost stagnant. The chiller did not come on line until April 1998, when renovations were nearly complete. When it warmed up outside, as it did a few times that spring, we could only dress for the heat and apologize to patrons.

Telephones presented another problem. The phone system at WL was overworked and outdated at best. With the onset of construction it became completely unreliable. For nearly six months we contended with a phone system that developed a series of different and frustrating illnesses each time construction crews removed walls or ran new wire. At one point none of the phone line lights in TAFKATS worked (we had old phones with lighted push buttons at the bottom to select a line). People could not tell whether someone was on a line, so they had to pick up, press a line button and listen or ask if anyone was already using that line. When a telephone rang, staff just kept pushing buttons until they found the line with the incoming caller. Incoming patron lines to the reference desk worked some days and not others. Since service desks moved more than once, library staff repeatedly had to reroute phone cords. (Duct tape is our friend, but gaff tape is better.) On good days the telephones worked fine. On bad days, the line lights did not come on, the hold button stopped working, phones in reference and youth services did not ring, and some departmental intercom numbers failed. Getting telephone lines or handsets repaired or even diagnosed in the midst of construction proved challenging also. When the phones broke on Thursday, they might not be fixed until Monday and then they would break again on Tuesday. The lights worked, but there was no dial tone and people calling in received a busy signal. At times the phone situation at WL became so convolutedly ill-functioning all we could do was laugh.

All departments had phone troubles during the renovation at WL. Usually they did not last more than a few days at a time. In the midst of them, however, patience was the only way of dealing with the problems. Most public service staff were rotated out to the JCCL on a set schedule, so they knew they would only be at WL for a matter of days or weeks before they could breathe the untroubled air of JCCL again.

Noise raised tension and blood pressures perhaps more than any other construction-related annoyance at WL, because so much of the construction activity occurred in enclosed areas or directly adjacent to them. Simultaneous projects all over the library made for noise pollution in every direction. Six months into the renovation, temporary walls were being constructed inside the adult and youth services areas, wall partitions for workrooms were going up, electrical and duct work was being done, and exterior demolition with jackhammers continued along with regular welding projects. Later, staff learned that noise levels would increase as a brick wall came down by reference and the concrete floors and stairs were jackhammered in old parts of the library. For patrons who found the noise too much, we handed out ear plugs to muffle the sound. Construction workers also took advantage of this unique patron perk. It was at this point that library staffers learned an important work world lesson. When welding smells became particularly noxious at one public service desk, staff insisted we call OSHA to see if some workplace rules were being violated. We appealed first to our wise and very safety-conscious construction manager, who assured us that "construction workers are people too," and that if there were dangerous substances involved, the construction crew wouldn't have been allowed to work around them either. We were duly chastened.

False fire and security alarms also plagued WL during the renovation project. There was virtually no way around it, because with workers constantly tinkering with wires, welding new seams and adding electrical outlets, putting up drywall, and changing untold other things, the alarm sensors were abused to the breaking point. The fire alarm was the most upsetting since its ear-splitting siren went off without warning and pulsed throughout the building. In one case the best solution was simply to disconnect the alarm sensor because anything less resulted in a false alarm every night. On workdays when the fire alarm was entirely disabled, e-mail was sent to all staff noting that if they saw a fire they should call 911, since pulling the alarm would be fruitless.

Not all stress in the building was directly construction-related, however. After phase two, the non-circulating reference collection was shifted to its new location by the adult reference staff in record time. Though the contractor promised three to five days to accomplish the task, as well as to transfer all the equipment, files, and books from the old reference desk

And the bricks came tumbling down at Williamsburg Library.

to the new one, while staff were calmly working out the details, they were abruptly informed that the move must be completed in a single morning.

The placement of each subject area, oversized titles, and periodical back files had been meticulously planned to insure a logical and easily understood arrangement for library patrons. Teams of two sprang into action, each provisioned with a book cart, to remove and transfer the books, while one librarian directed the traffic and controlled the spacing of Dewey ranges as well as multi-volume and growing series. The stacks had been equipped with six shelves. After shelving the first range, the staff discovered that too many books were taller than the allocated spaces. They fell to eliminating one shelf and repositioning the remaining five in each stack unit just in advance of the loaded book carts. They also interfiled the children's reference collection, which was to be housed in the adult area while the youth services department was closed during the last phase. At the end of a long, exhausting day the reference collection had been settled in its new home, beautifully positioned for use and expansion. The tired but joyful reference staff proudly displayed the results of their work to the director, who was equally joyful with one reservation. She pointed out that dog-eared telephone books and not pristine reference books immediately faced the windows fronting the busy street side of the building — a rather inelegant face for the new part of the library. The staff made adjustments the next day, and a lesson was learned about considering the "big picture."

Shifting, storing, and reshelving books was a never-ending task at WL during the project. In the adult area half the books had to be stored on temporary shelves in the basement (the Pit) during the renovation of the "old" adult services area. The other half of the adult collection, in the mezzanine, which was not undergoing extensive renovation, was left on the shelves but encapsulated in plastic for protection from dust and debris. Following phase two, when the adult stacks and adult reference area reopened, all the adult books that had been in storage returned upstairs and were replaced in the Pit by most of the youth services books. In the electronic catalog the agency of any stored books was batch changed to the invisible location of "boxed storage" (BS — yes, we did keep our sense of humor). This was to avoid patron frustration of seeing items listed that we could not physically access.

Soon after construction commenced on the expansion of the adult services area, construction also began at the other end of the building in youth services. Many children's librarians are known for their creativity. WRL's youth services staff are proud of their ability to morph any less than ideal situation into something productive, educational, or at minimum amusing.

Between erecting a new building and renovating another one, youth services staff felt as though they were caught in a never-ending construction zone. This affected everything they did, including summer reading. As JCCL was nearing completion, youth services learned that summer reading would coincide with the first phase of renovation at WL. The most visible impact was a large construction wall which would diminish the children's area. We reacted by developing a construction theme for summer reading. Staff wore hard hats and kids received child-sized hard hats as incentives. Summer reading participants also received cut-outs of construction vehicles and tools for the traditional mural, which we located on the construction wall. Construction personnel were even drafted to do storytimes. Our theme was called *Building Better Readers*. The children enjoyed the program, the library got wonderful publicity from local papers, and one construction manager will be fondly remembered by staff and children alike as Uncle Dunkle, storyteller extraordinaire. If you are going to have a construction project in the middle of your library's busiest season, you might as well use it to your advantage.

When all of the wires for computers and other equipment were brought down from the ceiling into the middle of the children's library to accommodate the construction wall, staff adapted the wires into a beanstalk. In order to keep little hands away from the wires they enclosed them in cardboard tubes. Then the tubes were decorated to resemble a large beanstalk. Half way up the stalk, staff created a small stuffed figure of a boy and lo and behold, Jack and his beanstalk were a new feature of the area. About a week later a custodian was working in the crawl space over the children's area when he stepped through two of the tiles, not hurting himself but leaving two large holes in the ceiling. A creative staff member made two large shoes to hang from the hole — the giant's feet. For the entire summer children came in and enjoyed our little tableau of Jack and the Beanstalk and the unfortunate giant.

In the early stages of the WL renovation we anticipated that the children's area would be closed for up to six months, so the challenge to youth services staff was to find a way to maintain as high a level of library service as possible for children in the area without a library space in Williamsburg. There would be service available at JCCL, but many people accustomed to using the Williamsburg Library were not yet convinced that JCCL was convenient, despite our arrangements with the accommodating public transit system for a stop at JCCL. To continue offering service in Williamsburg, we developed several options.

We organized a massive outreach program, taking storytimes to daycare centers, Head Start and anyplace else where kids gathered. We scheduled additional children's programs at JCCL instead of canceling programs that would have occurred at WL. To ensure we did not move books that would be discarded shortly after the renovation, youth services staff weeded the WL collection to within an inch of its life. Staff contacted local schools to be apprised of large upcoming homework assignments, pulled relevant materials, changed their status to non-circulating reference and shelved them in WL's newly opened adult section.

Then we realized we had a resource as yet overlooked. The library's old bookmobile had recently been replaced by a new, reliable bookmobile. The worn-out bookmobile had not yet found a home. Already set up to accommodate library materials, it was perfectly usable except as a moving vehicle. The retirement of the old bookmobile was cut short and it returned to serve as a remote facility we named the WRL Kids Book Xpress. The way we arrived at the name is another example of the fun we had keeping staff members involved. The youth services staff each submitted an idea to name the temporary bookmobile library, and a panel decided on the WRL Kids Book Xpress.

We contacted the owners of a small shopping center about a mile from WL and negotiated permission to park the bookmobile for the period of renovation. After countless conversations and negotiations of lease and liability forms, a temporary home for the old bookmobile was secured. Children's staff carefully selected 2,000 picture and juvenile fiction books. Automated services staff masked this collection in the electronic catalog, as they had done for the "boxed storage" collection, so staff could see the titles but patrons at WL and JCCL could not. Youth services staff shelved the small collection in the Kids Book Xpress. Then staff negotiated with the City of Williamsburg for temporary power and phone service at the spot in the shopping center where the bookmobile was parked.

Automated services used a laptop and with a combination of wizardry and persistence, set up an automated circulation system for the Xpress. Using a modem connection, the laptop provided access to the library's catalog and circulation modules, the Internet, and other networked resources. WRL's network administrator also used some inventive combinations of equipment to allow barcodes to be read and check-out receipts to be printed. For more technical details on the setup, please see the article published in *Computers in Libraries* magazine (April 1999). All youth services staff were trained in circulation functions at the check-out desk. First shift librarians performed the 11 step procedure to set up the laptop and test its connections in order to be ready for business in the morning. Staff working in the Xpress received permission to use the restrooms in a small department store in the shopping center.

By the time preparations were nearly complete, our cooperative contractor announced that the renovation work in youth services could be completed in only three months rather than six. We decided that the Book Xpress was still an excellent way to provide access to a sample of our collection for the kids in the area, and worth the work even for a relatively short period of time.

Flyers and press releases were sent out notifying the public of the closing of the children's area and the opening of the Kids Book Xpress. Our graphics manager made some wonderful banners to hang on the sides of the bookmobile, redesignating it the WRL Kids Book Xpress. On opening day the bookmobile manager coaxed one more trip out of the aging bookmobile from the library to the shopping center parking lot. Usage during its three-month run was not heavy, but those patrons who visited the Kids Book Xpress were loyal and grateful. One factor dissuading visits was that the Xpress had no heat. Even in southeastern Virginia, it gets cold in February and March. Large heating pads were purchased for staff to sit on and under to keep warm during shifts on the Xpress. On cold days, patrons tended to make their selections quickly, and leave, rather than lingering to chat.

To our amusement, some people misunderstood why the bookmobile was parked in the shopping center parking lot. When several staff wearing their name tags went to a restaurant in the shopping center for lunch, their server mentioned how sorry she was that our bookmobile had broken down in the parking lot.

The Kids Book Xpress, in its limited role, worked very well. It was a public relations and public service hit. Perhaps the best part is that as a result of the Xpress project the old bookmobile found a new home. A small neighboring library system liked our example and negotiated for the old vehicle when the children's area reopened at WL. The WRL Board of Trustees agreed to pass it on to our neighbor, who used it to set up a permanent book station in a part of their service area where there had been no library outlet before.

Library staff were also pleased that in spite of the upheaval caused by the construction and renovations at WL, the entire facility closed to the public for only 10 days, and most of that occurred in December, the slowest time of the year for us, and a period which would have included holiday closings anyway. For several weeks before we closed, circulation staff extended due dates so that no items would be due while the library was closed. During that time, staff moved the check-out and reference desks to the newly renovated areas of the library and got shelving areas ready for the second phase of construction. Items could be returned at the book drop or taken to JCCL. Because the arts center entrance is separate from the rest of the library, the closing did not completely halt meeting room reservations or use of the Williamsburg Library Theatre; in addition, patrons could pick up their reserve books from 10 to 5 on weekdays at the arts center entrance.

Throughout the process, many patrons seemed to understand that we were doing our best to shield them from as much inconvenience as we could. Patrons were as likely to express their sympathy about what the staff were going through as they were to complain about the upheaval.

WL closed twice in February for a total of nine days. Construction crews needed part of that time to take down the largest of the temporary walls. The second closing allowed staff to move the adult books back to their permanent shelves and move children's books to the Pit. These disruptions to service were minimal enough to not cause much concern among patrons, again because staff planned well to continue critical services even when we were closed. During the February closings, reference staff made sure that boxes of the most often requested tax forms were left in foyers that were open 24 hours a day.

Providing public service with a smile in a construction area is not easy. WRL staff did it by planning well and focusing on the positive — soon we would have a beautifully enlarged library to present to the community. We also tried to find humor in any situation. Youth services spent a month dressed in winter coats, hats, and gloves, sitting on heating pads to stay warm. They could have complained about it constantly, but laughing was more fun.

Other instances we chose to find humor in include the time program services staff moved their entire operation onto a card table with a typing chair for about a week, while crews jackhammered a conduit through the concrete floor. A man who was almost arrested for trespassing early one morning was just acting on a request from his wife; she wanted cuttings from a tree inside the construction fence. There were also many e-mails that unintentionally turned out to be funny, at least to us. "What's that smell at WL?" was an unintended rhyme that gave us a chuckle to savor that day.

Seemingly straightforward events sometimes turned into wonderful anecdotes. One example was when the construction liaison, for the second or third time in a week, was dragged out of bed early in the morning to respond to a false alarm. When she arrived a construction worker was explaining to a police officer that he had entered the code, but the alarm went off anyway. She reset the system and returned outside to sign the police report. The officer suggested that she might want to go home and

**Construction fence at Williamsburg Library.**

catch a quick nap before coming back to work for the day. As she wrote in an e-mail later that day, "I thought that was nice since he'd been on duty all night, but I couldn't figure out why he thought I was so tired. When I got home, I understood his concern. I had my clothes on inside out! I went back to bed and took a quick nap and now I'm here clothed correctly. There is truly humor in everything and I got my first laugh of the day early. Hope this gives you one too." To get the most out of a renovation project, you must use your sense of humor and approach each day as an adventure — because it will be one, so you might as well enjoy it.

# 5

# Dealing with
# Construction Professionals

For both the JCCL construction project and the WL renovation project, the library director appointed a staff member to act as a liaison with construction professionals. In the case of JCCL it was mostly our circulation services director. For WL it was the collection services director. Both people acted as the main contact for library staff in regard to questions about the construction concerns and for construction staff in regard to questions about library needs. Their construction duties were added onto their regular duties, so they had lots more work to do, but they certainly learned a lot of new things—and new words. Luckily for WRL, both of our liaisons were able to handle the additional workload without complaint, because they were excited about the construction projects and eager to learn more about the process.

When James City County purchased the building site for a library and design work began, our technical services director became the library's liaison on the project. She never had been good at turning down challenging projects so she accepted this one too; in addition, since technical services operations were to be headquartered at JCCL, she had a vested interest in the project.

One of her first efforts was to arrange a series of meetings in which she and the architects and designers met with each department to discuss department desk and workroom designs, staff requests, decorative issues and the like. For issues that overlapped departments, such as acquisitions and opening day collection planning, representatives from the involved departments met with construction coordinators, when appropriate, to organize how everything would eventually come together.

Eight months after the design work began, she left WRL for a post in California. At that point, the library director took over project management. Fortunately for us, the technical services director returned as head of circulation and again assumed her role as liaison for the construction of JCCL. She had missed a year's worth of effort, which included the groundbreaking and the concrete slab being poured. With the library director, our new head of circulation began attending weekly project meetings in the construction trailer at the building site. That experience taught them a good number of lessons about communicating with the parties involved.

Project meetings usually included the architect, often the interior designer, the county's project manager, the county's engineering consultant, and the contractor's project manager. Occasionally subcontractors such as the painter or the concrete worker would attend as well. The meetings were well-organized and consisted of three to fifteen items of immediate interest: What color concrete? Tell us again which windows should open? My guys need to get to work, when is that sheetrock going to be up? Who took delivery of those bookdrops that came in four months early, and where did they put them? The staff liaison listened to it all and took detailed notes, made easier by the architect's meeting agenda. If a decision was required, she or the library director could make it right then so no contractor would have to wait. If a decision required further information, the liaison made sure we got the architect and project manager the information in a timely fashion. Or, if the ball was in someone else's court, she made sure we at the library got a copy of the information or decision. During the JCCL project, the fax machine was our best friend. By the time of the WL renovation, both the fax machine and e-mail had become indispensable. During the WL renovation, the library's liaison also met with the director and the construction professionals, usually once a month. The project manager provided the agendas, which included standard construction questions as well as CBIs (crybaby issues).

For JCCL, James City County appointed one of their employees to be the project manager, and hired a clerk of the works, so the county had a staff person on site during construction. The City of Williamsburg hired an outside construction management (CM) firm — Gilbane Building Company — for the WL expansion project. The CM's primary role was to represent our interests in renovating the building, and we got an excellent project manager. He oversaw all aspects of the construction, from pouring concrete and putting up walls to ordering building materials and getting walls painted the right colors.

While writing this book, library staff have done a lot of reflection on the construction process. We thought it would be instructive to ask the construction management team for WL to do the same thing, so we asked

Project manager Bernie Farmer, Clerk of the Works Fletcher Frye, and program services director Patrick Golden inspect James City County Library.

our project manager (Greg Dunkle) and his supervisor (Andy Faber, the project executive) a series of questions about the WL renovation project. The answers reveal something about construction professionals in general, as well as the perspectives held by professionals at different levels of the corporate ladder. Here are the questions and their answers.

*1. What does a project executive do on this sort of project?*

**Andy:** The Project Executive's role on this type of assignment is to make sure our company is providing the services we are contracted to provide at the highest level of quality. In addition my role is to be certain our jobsite is getting the support they need from the regional office in an effort to provide quality service.

**Greg:** On a project such as Williamsburg City Complex, as GBCo called it, a PX [project executive] is fairly removed until such time that a situation warrants or client management is needed. As an impartial third party a PX may lend an objective opinion to a topic which has been stale or in a stalemate. This occurred once during my term at the library.

*2. Your company has worked on the Library of Virginia as well as on our library project, and we know you're famous for your work on prisons and jails. So, what do you see as the similarities and differences between jails and libraries?*

> **Andy:** There are no similarities between jails and libraries. All construction projects are, however, constructed by people out of "bricks and mortar" in strict compliance with the plans and specifications. All projects have architects and engineers and most importantly, owners. The one similarity all projects have is that our role as a CM (Construction Manager) is to see that the project is built in strict accordance with the plans and specifications on time and within budget. Library clients are typically not well versed in construction and require more "hand holding" than prison clients.

> **Greg:** I was not on the Library of Virginia job, but as far as jails and libraries, I think the bars are a big difference. I would say that seriously they are both in the public eye because they are funded by tax dollars. This puts them on a pedestal for being critiqued by the public in general. The differences are easy, people welcome libraries for the most part and jails/prisons are usually not well received. The construction process is similar in all projects. Just the materials and end result change.

*3. What exactly does a construction management firm do? What does the construction management firm bring to the relationship among the owner (and the occupant when the occupant is not the owner), the architect, and the general contractor, etc.?*

> **Andy:** A CM firm is typically hired to represent the owner's interest in constructing a building. The CM is in an advocacy role and is hired solely to see that the owner's objectives of cost, quality and schedule are achieved. The CM should be the "driving force" behind the project and develop relationships of trust and mutual respect between the owner, the user, and the architect so the project can be built in an atmosphere of partnership.

> **Greg:** The CM firm is brought into a project for various reasons. When an owner is about to undertake a large construction project, the CM can lend valuable advice, assistance and services throughout the pre-planning, design review, bidding, construction and closeout of a job. With an objective look CMs provide feedback for the various opinions of all players within a team. A sort of Captain of the team. With the Owner mainly fixed on cost and schedule, the Tenant [this was the

library, in our project] emphasizing technology and functionality, the Architect concerned with form and aesthetics, and the Contractor based on his cost and ease of construction, one could see how an outsider may be needed to mesh all the opinions and provide guidance to the team. The above is an illustration and of course some of the focuses do change in different projects.

*4. What are the major differences between working on new construction and working on projects involving additions/renovations?*

**Andy:** Renovations are more challenging due to working in an existing facility where changed conditions happen daily. In addition, working close to an occupied building requires logistical planning that everyone must buy into for the job to run smoothly. Safety of the public is also a major concern in working in or around an occupied facility.

**Greg:** Renovations and new construction both have their little secrets which are uncovered along the way. The major difference would be the occupation of the building during construction. This is a major concern for ensuring safety of the patrons in the case of the Williamsburg Library. The involvement of having an on site owner is valuable to ensure that the project is progressing towards the final requirements of the end user.

*5. Was there anything particularly interesting about the Williamsburg Library project (that you can talk about in print)?*

**Andy:** What was interesting to me was seeing how effective a young engineer [Greg] could be in providing services purely due to his ability to deal with people. This is truly a people business. Also interesting was the lack of trust between the owner, the user and the architect and how Gilbane bridged that gap.

**Greg:** The group that I got to work with were great. Everyone took everything in stride, a lot better than I had expected. It was neat having a group of people so interested in the project. We usually get so buried in the details we don't get to see the people's faces light up at progress and the end result.

*6. Can you explain the difference between a project engineer, a project manager and a project executive?*

**Andy:** The project executive has overall responsibility for several projects. A project manager reports to the project executive and is our lead person on site. A project engineer reports to the project manager and is typically responsible for the "paper work" such as submittals, shop drawings, reports, and change order management. On very small contracts, the project engineer may replace the project manager. This is how we were set up on your project.

**Greg:** $30k each stage. One does everything, one watches everything being done, one takes credit for everything.

*7. Is it hard not to become emotionally involved in a project? Is there a danger to becoming emotionally involved?*

**Andy:** Construction is a very risky and stressful business. Any time you have those factors involved it is difficult not to become emotional. This is ok ... the key is to keep your emotions in check and don't lose sight of the big picture goal of what you are trying to accomplish. The key emotion is to remain intensely dedicated to that goal and tough minded about achieving it. You must however always remain calm.

**Greg:** Everything which is done should be done in moderation. I believe a certain amount of emotion is good for a project. Enough emotion to keep it interesting and to keep the client's concerns first and foremost. Not enough to keep one up at night.

*8. What are the most important attributes of a good construction manager/management firm? A good client? A good architect? A good contractor?*

**Andy:** It is all about people ... people ... people!!! Also having integrity and a proper mission statement. Having passion for what you do and passing that to people is key in all businesses. A good owner makes timely decisions and recognizes the challenges of construction and is willing to invest in a relationship of trust with the CM and architect.

**Greg:** CM — experience in all types of building, common sense, interpersonal skills. Client — Open mind and ability to be flexible. Also empowering a point of contact for decision making. Architect — Same as above, interpersonal skills are a must when working with the Client. Contractor — Flexibility and understanding; they are at the bottom of the food chain and start the next one.

*9. Even when employing a construction management firm, the owner/occupant still must know some things to make certain that the project turns out well. What are the three most important things you think the owner/occupant needs to know?*

**Andy:** See answer to question 8.

**Greg:** (1) Concept of time and work to be completed within that time; (2) The work most likely will encounter cost and possibly schedule impacts; (3) the process can be a learning experience and does not have to be painful.

*10. What are the three important items for the owner/occupant to consider in planning a construction project?*

**Andy:** Hire a good architect, hire a good CM and have contingency funds available to pay for problems you will encounter. Leave yourself enough time to do the job and get the CM involved very early in the process.

**Greg:** (1) Cost; (2) Schedule; (3) Quality of Finishes and Material Selections. All three of the above interact with one another. If the schedule gets shorter the cost gets larger or the quality of materials goes down. If the quality of materials is to increase so will the price or the schedule. If you reduce cost you must reduce quality of materials or scope. The above three should only be considered after establishing well defined program requirements for the project.

One important point that both men make is that construction is a business, and that things can take longer and cost more than you expect. That is why both Greg and Andy suggested contingency funds and flexibility; we point this out because public libraries and their municipalities usually shy away from large "contingency funds" or anything else that sounds like over-budgeting. Greg's and Andy's responses assert that contingency plans should be part of the process, not an optional line in the budget. Nor should the comment about construction being about people be underestimated. Construction workers are people and appreciate being treated with respect, just as library workers do. They have numerous stresses of which we may not be aware, even though they are tied to our construction project. It is very important that construction supervisors and library staff know who can make decisions. Gilbane's project engineer/manager was very good at keeping the construction supervisors aware that only he and the library's liaison to the project could make critical decisions. At JCCL we were warned that when construction workers needed an answer, they'd ask anybody who walked by, hoping to get a quick, easy answer. Library staff were warned not to answer such requests, but inevitably some did, fortunately not with any irreversible results.

Andy's comment about the lack of "trust" we exhibited is interesting to us. From our perspective it was a healthy skepticism that had developed as a result of experience and that ensured that what we asked for was going to be built. In both construction projects, we found that the more questions we asked, the more likely we got what we wanted or at least what was possible. Listen and learn, ask questions simply and directly; if you aren't sure how to ask a question, preface it with some kind of good-natured caveat. Pretend you're the patron and the architect is the librarian, and ask a question the way you'd want to be asked. We discovered that if you shy away from learning the construction process, you concede much of your ability to articulate your goals. Fortunately, our project manager seemed to understand this and was very willing to help us learn. He was also very good about warning us as much in advance as possible when significant construction disruptions were approaching. By the midpoint of the project, we knew he was just as committed to it as we were.

Architects are wonderful people. We liked all the architects we worked with very much. However, we learned that it was best to approach our relationship with the architect as one of friendly adversaries. Our goals did not always coincide, and we learned to be assertive in making our wishes known. At JCCL, especially in youth services, the architect did not always appreciate our priorities. During the design process at JCCL, the library director spent much of one meeting convincing the architect's team that we did not want a room divider in the large meeting room. Only later did we learn that the divider recommended would have cost $30,000 — the designer hadn't even mentioned the cost during his recommendation.

At WL, we had a more difficult relationship with the architect, particularly on one part of the project. The architect was contracted to provide the interior design team. The arrangement is common on this sort of project, but did not work well for us. Interior design is an important component of any library construction project, and we did our best to work with the original interior designer, who had no library experience and was less than enthusiastic about listening to those of us who did.

Repeatedly, for almost a year, we brought our concerns about the design team to the attention of the architect. After presenting many examples of misinformation, including incorrect and inflated pricing information, unwillingness to provide copies of relevant building codes that would affect the library interior, and unwillingness to accept our decisions not to pursue specific ideas (examples: not repainting existing shelving and eliminating a large central light fixture that was quickly dubbed the "snake light"), the library director wrote a memorandum to the architect detailing our problems. WL staff had taken to working around the interior design team, consulting directly with supplier companies to get answers and accurate information. The director noted, "You get the idea they don't know who the client is." The interior designer's lack of respect for the library's construction liaison was the final straw. The director stated that WRL staff would not participate in any additional meetings with the design team unless the architect was present.

When the architect asserted that the communication problems rested solely with library staff, we were at an impasse. The library liaison took over the interior design responsibilities, learned a lot in the process, and got a much better product for less money than the architect's estimates. Amazingly, the shelf painting and the snake light still made their way into the construction documents. With the aid of friendly construction staff, we were able to identify them early enough in the process to eliminate them and save even more money.

This experience made it apparent that library staff must make priorities clear from the beginning, watch like a hawk at each step, and still not be surprised if we don't get what we asked for. It's not that construction professionals are bad people, or even indifferent — they seemed to think they were protecting us from ourselves.

To further appreciate the experience of construction professionals, we asked Bernard Farmer, who was the county's construction manager on the JCCL project, to write a few words. His text follows.

## *Construction Management*

Construction management can be defined as the administration, direction, and management of a construction project. This is a simplistic though all-encompassing definition for a complex activity that involves many groups, lots of money, great risks, and much opportunity for failure. When done well, all parties in the process benefit greatly. When done poorly, the results have a demonstrable cost to the owner, the architect, the contractor, and the community.

The term "construction management" has in recent times been used to describe a wide variety of actions that could solve every possible hazard inherent in the building process. Firms that specialize in this work have hyped their abilities; while at the same time attempted to avoid any responsibility for any of the many pitfalls inherent in the process. Practitioners of "construction management" can be anyone from an attorney, architect, owner, contractor, independent consultant, or nearly anyone else involved in the trades. The American Institute of Architects (AIA),

Associated General Contractors of America (AGC), and the Construction Management Association of America (CMAA) all have published standard documents that can constitute the standard form of agreement between an owner and a "construction manager" (CM). Any of these standard forms could form a basis for developing an agreement to perform the construction management duties, depending on the desires of the owner.

An examination of developments in the construction industry can help to explain how construction management has risen to its current position of prominence. Some issues to consider are:

- Design professionals make every attempt possible to distance themselves from directing, supervising, inspecting, or coordinating the construction process.
- Technological advances continue to introduce specialized systems and materials into projects, making them more difficult to coordinate and direct due to the number and complexity of specialty items and contractors.
- Public owners desire greater efficiencies, and citizen groups demand more accountability than ever before.
- No single entity involved in the process is vested in the overall success of the total project to the extent of the owner; rather each is interested in his own little piece and not how it combines with everyone else's efforts.

Consequently, it becomes apparent that the responsibility to coordinate various procurements, schedule complex and sometimes conflicting activities, remain concerned with project efficiencies to prevent unnecessary expense and delay regardless of who is responsible (note that most contractors aren't worried about a delay caused by someone else, as it gives them a great excuse for future defense), and control overall project costs is assumed by no single entity on the job. Thus the concept of a construction manager arose to fill this void.

How an owner provides the work for construction management can take many forms, from hiring large national firms with extensive qualifications to simply appointing an existing employee. Regardless of the choice, any owner should follow some simple steps to minimize confusion and add clarity. First and foremost the owner should detail the responsibilities and liabilities of the CM in a concise and appropriate agreement. Second, the duties ascribed to the CM should not be in conflict with those of the architect or contractor. The CM is not an additional designer sent to a project site that can overrule the design of the architect. In the same light, the CM has no place in directing the work of a subcontractor on the job, but rather must still rely on the prime contractor to perform his duties. Finally, if the CM is a firm or entity hired, the owner should require adequate financial responsibility, performance bond, or insurance that covers any risk allocated to the CM.

Under the strictest legalistic view, an owner's responsibilities under the terms of the AIA standard agreements can be boiled down to two simple tasks. Those are, pay for work per the terms of the agreement, and don't delay the actions of the contractor. However, we all know much more is required for a successful project. Work toward this success begins at the outset of project conception, and doesn't end until long after the building is occupied. It is in the owner's most basic interests to become actively involved, engaged, and informed throughout the entire project, regardless of what services have been hired.

While the work goes well beyond the construction period, this section will concern itself primarily with duties once a contractor has been selected to do a project, and an outline will be presented that is one model for a successful project.

Any construction activity ultimately involves humans and their interaction. By their very nature, people respond much better in an environment of involvement as opposed to detachment. People give more of themselves when they feel ownership and partnership. Given these simplistic truisms, it defies logic to think that the building "team" doesn't involve more than the contractors, but must include the subcontractors, principal designers, owners, material suppliers, and other vested parties. The first step of any construction activity must involve an investment toward forming that partnership and human relationship that will carry throughout the job. The owner should seek commitment that people will work toward the common goal of a successful project. The owner should also attempt to identify those areas where conflict might exist. This exercise of developing interpersonal relationships, defining roles, and identifying opportunities for resolution of conflict can take many forms, depending upon the complexity of a project. In more complex projects, an investment in a consultant that performs "partnering" or "team building" exercises for the construction industry should be considered. These trained facilitators can tailor their presentations and exercises to the specific project at hand. Regardless of the form, the owner's first task must be to recognize the importance of human interaction in the process and attempt to build upon the strength of an involved relationship.

It has often been said that a person who doesn't know where he is going may never know when he is lost. In the same vein, lack of a plan doesn't give one the right to claim success with any outcome. Success on most any construction project will be defined by completion of work on time, within budget, and to a standard defined within the plans and specifications. These three elements of time, budget, and quality form the basis for management of any project and will be addressed in greater detail below.

The single most important tool for monitoring time on a project involves the construction schedule. The question of who should prepare and maintain the schedule can be debated, but must be clearly defined under the terms of the construction contract. In my experience, preparation and update by the contractor, subject to approval by the owner or CM, is the best method. The contractor knows best what forces are available to perform work, what sequence he desires for various activities, and is in the position to direct subcontractors to start work on various activities. However, the owner should review, question, and require modification of any schedule if they find errors of fact, omission of activities, overly aggressive or optimistic work times, or problems of logic sequence.

The form of the schedule can be anything from a simple list to a complex matrix, but the most common practice is to use the critical path method (CPM) schedule. In this method, activities are organized and linked based upon starting and end dates and a detailed analysis of construction sequencing. Preparation of the schedule requires technical expertise, construction judgement, and some common sense gained from practical experience. Both early start/end and normal start/end dates are assigned, based upon an analysis of how an activity fits into the process, and duration of each activity is determined. When all activities are linked together, certain activities will become critical to the end date of the work; that is, any addition of time to their start or end dates will change the overall project completion date. Hence, these activities are deemed the "critical path" and deserve the greatest attention during the project. Note, however, other activities not on the critical path can become "critical activities" if the late start dates are exceeded. Consequently, preparation of an accurate forecast at the outset, constant attention to the activities during the progress of the work, and continuous update during the project are all important elements of time management. Some considerations to make in planning any project are:

• What frequency of update to the schedule will be required?
• Who must review and approve any schedule or update?

- Is the presentation of an update tied to any request for payment?
- What actions must the contractor take if he gets off schedule?

Finally, the owner must state in the contract and at the outset of the job, as well as throughout the project, that schedule is important and adherence to the published schedule is an absolute requirement for successful completion of the work.

# 6

# Technology Upgrades

Both of WRL's construction projects offered tremendous opportunities to expand the electronic resources that we could provide for patrons and staff.

The James City County Library became the foundation upon which WRL could build its technological pyramid. Included in the JCCL designs were rooms, conduits, connection points and the like to accommodate the latest technology and shepherd WRL into the twenty-first century. We've described a bit of the process in other parts of the book, but here it is in more detail.

At JCCL, before any new equipment arrived, preparation for installation began. The first step was to install the hundreds of feet of cable needed to serve our computer, voice, and modem networks. The library's systems administrator acted as the liaison with Net100, the cabling contractor, to inform them when different parts of the building would be ready for cabling. Although the Herman Miller modular office panels we selected to create work spaces could have accommodated our cables, we opted to use connection boxes flush with the wall. This was a decision based on future flexibility we stood up for despite the fact that all the construction professionals and both county project managers thought the connection boxes would result in messy nests of cables under each desk. We wanted to use the connection boxes on the wall, because if the contractor had run the wire directly from the wall through the furniture, it would have been much more difficult for library staff to move our own furniture in the future.

Anyway, each wall box accommodated six cable connections—data, voice, or modem. Each type of connection used a different color wall jack for easy visual identification — blue for data, green for modem, and black for voice. We also added word labels ("data," "modem," "voice") to idiot-proof the building. (That's another thing we learned; no matter how saturated your brain feels with construction information, you will probably forget it as soon as you move in and start really using the building.) To reduce costs, Category 5 cable was used only for computer network connections; we used regular telephone wire for the modem and telephone connections. With the cable in place, face plates were installed. The library's project liaison also lobbied for (and got) white face plates. The architect, while designing a beautiful, clean-looking, modern building, had specified the perpetually dirty-looking ivory face plates. Automated services staff marked each face plate with a unique number that corresponded to the location on the planning spreadsheet and to the matching jack in one of the computer rooms. Using the spreadsheet, automated services staff installed shorter patch cables to connection jacks where PCs and dumb terminals would later be placed. Patch cables are what you use between your computer and the wall. The jack numbering scheme was used to number the patch cables as well, helping ensure easy identification once office panels were up. Pulling patch cables under the panels rather than threading them through the panel's wire troughs meant less cable was needed and that any future redesign of space would not require significant effort to move panels or cables. Telephone line cords and modem cords were similarly pre-installed in areas where office panels would block access to wall connection boxes. The master spreadsheet also provided a check-off sheet for automated services staff and the county's project manager to use to verify that all connections contracted for were correctly placed.

After office panels had been assembled to create work spaces, we began installing equipment. As each piece of equipment arrived, it was marked with a library inventory number and entered into a database created by automated services staff. The type of equipment, serial number, purchase date, vendor, and equipment specifications were recorded. The building and department to which the computer equipment was assigned and any known problems with the equipment were also added as appropriate. The database, which we've continued to use for our subsequent purchases, provides an immediate snapshot of equipment in each building, by department, denotes equipment under warranty, identifies types or models of equipment that were problematic, and even flags vendors whose equipment has been substandard. The planning spreadsheet guided automated services staff on where to place computer terminals and peripherals in each work space and helped keep organized the hundreds of PCs, printers, uninterruptible power supplies (UPSs) and modems that arrived within a few days of one another.

The final step in this process was installing software at each workstation and setting up connections to our library network. While certain programs were common to all the new PCs and had been loaded by the vendor, additional packages had to be loaded and configured at certain workstations. The spreadsheet confirmed for us that we had adequate licenses for the installations we performed and that programs were installed where they were needed. It was around this time that there were several news stories about nonprofits that had gotten into hot water by not having enough licenses for all the copies of programs they were using, so we were happy to be able to keep (and show) track of ours.

With the completion of JCCL, the next priority was public access to the Internet. Surfing the Internet has been likened by some as an adventure for anyone willing to take the challenge. As it turned out for us, just gaining access to the Internet was an adventure in itself.

At his first meeting with an outside vendor, our very new network administrator listened to a presentation by a salesman pitching his company's turnkey Internet system. The library's goal was to get the two buildings on the Internet. We already had a network set up that connected the sister libraries, but there was no public access to the Internet and this was something we all wanted to achieve. The public was beginning to expect this resource, so we were feeling the pressure to come online as soon as possible. The salesman ended his pitch with a price quote of just over $60,000, plus an annual maintenance fee of $1,800. The system came with free software too. Unaccustomed to bandying about five figure price tags, the network administrator let out an audible gasp when he heard the amount. But after he had patiently listened to the entire presentation without comment, he pointed out that much of the "bonus" software could be downloaded from the Internet for free. All the salesman could stammer was that his system came all ready to plug in and go online.

We were being offered a remarkable product, but one that was intended for an organization that did not have budget restrictions and did not care that it was getting a system that was tremendously overpowered. The salesman offered a Sparc 20 machine. As our network administrator put it, Sparcstations were the things that geeks dreamed about. A Sparc 20 was an extremely powerful machine for extremely serious situations— tracking subatomic particles as they cross the sun, and things like that. We did not need that kind of capability. We needed a pickup truck and we were offered an 18–wheeler that would easily support up to 1,000 users. At the time, we had only 140 users, counting staff and public PCs.

WRL was extremely fortunate to have a network administrator who had worked nearly a year at a local Internet service provider (ISP). He was there when the business started and saw all the problems and confusion that came with learning about a burgeoning technology. While he understood that the technology could get complicated, he also knew that the library's cash flow was not this rich. The salesman was trying to sell us something we could not afford and did not need. The meeting ended and the salesman left. We did not invest $60,000 to achieve connectivity.

Our network administrator developed an alternate solution — one that cost the library about one-twelfth of what the salesman had suggested. Unwilling to blindly accept the turnkey-but-it's-gonna-cost-you mentality, he considered his options. He was faced with the seemingly opposed properties of a small budget and the need for a reliable system. We wanted to do the Internet on a realistic, sustainable budget, not on a shoestring. Again, the previous experience of our network administrator proved invaluable. He knew the local Internet service provider had avoided the high-end computer operating systems that most ISPs use. The first thing the network administrator did was select a complete Internet–ready operating system called Linux. One of its best features is that Linux is not particular about what brand of computer it runs on. Alternatives like Sparcstations, Hewlett-Packards and IBMs all work only with the manufacturer's operating system. The computer and the software are purchased together as a package deal, leaving some software users at the mercy of companies with poor technical support. The users cannot afford to change operating systems since that requires changing hardware, which effectively means starting from scratch. It is clearly a cost prohibitive prospect. Linux required no particular computer — a regular desktop personal computer worked fine. That appealed to the network administrator, because it meant that when hardware broke (as it always does) the library could get replacement parts locally and install them without help from hardware service people with system specific expertise.

Another equally appealing aspect of Linux was its cost. It was created in Finland by a student, Linus Torvalds. He wanted to develop an operating system that was free of corporate dominance and free of their controls and limitations. (Kind of like the public library.) And one that was free of cost. Anyone willing to learn how to use it can download Linux from the Internet without cost. Mr. Torvalds made it that way on purpose.

If a local ISP could start with a slightly hot-rodded personal computer as the base of their operations, WRL could try, too. So, taking advantage of the network administrator's expertise and Linux's availability, WRL built its own Internet server. Rather than spend $60,000 on a prefabricated system, we were able to screw something together on our own — starting with a desktop computer.

With the surrender of one desktop computer to the cause, the network administrator and his part-time computer technician took on the project. The network administrator promised to have the system up and running in a month or he'd restore the PC to its original state — then acquiesce and buy the virtual farm, $60,000 dollar price tag and all. What library director would not agree to that experiment? It was a good time (for the network administrator) to remember the ever-so-sage advice: be careful what you ask for, you might get it.

The project started with a desktop computer as promised — a garden variety PC: Pentium 100 Mhz with 16 megabytes of RAM, and a 1.2 gigabyte hard disk. The technician immediately suggested replacing the hard disk with a much faster and larger Small Computer System Interface drive (SCSI, pronounced "scuzzy" by computer geeks). Linux allows many people to use the computer at the same time, but the storebought hard drive was not designed for that. SCSI drives come with, effectively, their own dedicated computer that acts as a traffic officer to all the processing that users generate when they log onto the system to, for instance, check e-mail. Even 20 people all checking their e-mail simultaneously creates a lot of data coming and going; so would 100.

The network administrator asked for what was to be the single biggest expense — $800 for one main hard drive and a backup, just in case. He also thought to boost the RAM in the machine to 32 megabytes, which cost another $200. He could have used the PC as it was, but decided to improve the chance of success by improving the power of the machine since it would be required to manage the Internet service of an entire institution. Besides, if it failed, the administrator figured he could return all the hardware for a refund within 30 days.

It later became clear that the bottleneck in access speed with most network servers, storebought or otherwise, is almost always limited by the hard drive. More memory, faster processing, and even a faster network all around makes less difference on the user's end compared to a fast hard drive in the server. Upgrading anything else first does not speed things up if the data is slow to rise to the surface when it is needed.

One important detail the salesman neglected to mention in his initial pitch, and something that was needed before going any further with this homemade server idea, was a full-time connection to the Internet. Without an Internet connection it is like building a really nice phone, but not having anyplace to get a dial tone. We should say here that our network administrator has a special gift for explaining technical things in terms any manager can understand. If you don't have such a person on staff, we're sorry.

It is probable that had WRL purchased the Sparcstation system it would have come with the recommendation to lease a circuit from the telephone company, at around $1,000 a month. That type of connection could have provided incredible speed, but also would have been more than an institution such as WRL, just getting started in the online world, needed. Perhaps in time WRL could really use (and pay for) such a thing, but small steps seemed the best choice for an infant system. The library's needs could be met with something much more modest.

Enter the owner of a second local Internet service provider (not the one where the network administrator had worked, incidentally). It was the good fortune of WRL that the provider's kids loved visiting the Williamsburg Library. It was time to find out whether he would be interested in donating a medium-speed connection to the Internet. The answer was yes. Ben Loyall, owner of Widomaker Communications Services, Inc., brought our network administrator an ISDN modem and offered to loan it to the library free of charge for the duration of our connection through Widomaker. This type of modem was, at the time, the kind that at-home Internet speed demons craved. The loan of the modem was generous in itself, but he also was willing to set up an ISDN modem at Widomaker Communications and, most important of all, absorb the monthly bill for the phone company to run the special circuit between Widomaker and WRL to make it all happen. Through this conduit all of the library's Internet access would flow, including e-mail coming and going and web page traffic. In essence it became the library pipeline to the outside virtual world and it was all tax deductible for Mr. Loyall.

Admittedly, the connection was not tremendously fast. But it was adequate. It gave WRL 118K speed, which was about five times as fast as most standard telephone modems. Considering this would make it possible to offer five Internet workstations to the public and that our staff of 100 was brand new to the Internet and did not do a lot of surfing to begin with, it worked quite well. In fact, it was more than a year and a half, during which five more public Internet workstations and many more staff members came online, before we decided that WRL had outgrown this initial setup.

The technical details of how WRL got its Internet server up and running are too complicated to try to narrate here (and quite possibly outdated with the quick progression of technology). Suffice it to say, that once it was working, it worked very dependably. And, without the advice and aid provided by people around the world it would have been impossible. Even after the able computer technician moved on to another position, leaving the network administrator to steer a course alone, there was almost always a fellow Linux user online he could call on for help or advice.

This is the catch–22 associated with using the Linux operating system: most of the support assistance available comes from users online.

Without a way to connect to the Internet when help was needed, the network administrator would have been lost. He already had procured such a connection from a local ISP, but even if he'd been forced to purchase a commercial account for the 30 days of the server experiment, it would have been worth the investment. There is a wealth of information about Linux on the Internet and you must have access to this if you are going to make things work.

Without corporate ties or an associated license (so far), Linux has been adopted by a great number of programmers and engineers who have made it their own — literally. Originally designed to be modular in nature, some folks have made portions of the Linux operating system their specialty. One person might be a hard drive whiz and someone else might concentrate on modems. And since this is a definite labor of love on their part, they are often willing to supply documentation that is surprisingly understandable to non-experts. This was one of Linus Torvald's goals with Linux and it has been beautifully realized in the giving spirit of these dedicated computer folks.

In any case, we rarely had to directly contact one of these digital gurus. If the documentation did not provide enough help when a problem came up, the network administrator discovered that other Linux users had probably had the same thing happen to them. He could record the error message and then enter it into a search engine. He had the best luck searching the news groups and with his favorite search engine, www.deja.com. It's amazing how many times the exact solution appears from a simple search.

All of this should not be taken to imply that working with Linux is always easy. Our homemade Linux Internet server was a real challenge to get going at first. For a while, it was a bigger challenge keeping it going. But it got better as we learned more and all in all WRL's Internet server and operating system has been more dependable than our catalog was when first installed. The server handled e-mail for over 100 staff members, our homepage, and several other network functions for about 30 months. Total down time was around 3 percent.

WRL was hacked twice during that time. The first time the unwelcome "guest" simply locked up the server and backups came to the rescue. The second time someone outside took control, they decided to use our little computer as a platform from which to launch attacks on another server that belonged to a financial institution in Chicago. WRL received cease and desist e-mail from the latter, and they seemed satisfied that we were simple victims in the whole affair.

Both of these hacking events could have been prevented by keeping all the Linux software on the server up to date. Keeping a server secure is not unlike keeping a door secure: you build a better lock, the bad guys learn to pick it, so you build an even better lock, and they learn to pick that. Gratefully, those digital gurus take responsibility for building the better locks and all a network administrator has to do is install them. Once ours discovered where to look for the updates, the successful hacking stopped.

Obviously, WRL did not buy the $60,000 server. The homespun effort, with its $1,000 of extras, and the time it took to figure it all out have worked quite well. And we used the $60,000 for something special, like books.

# SECTION III

*Living with the Results*

# 7

# Opening Day Events and the Realities of Your Facilities

For JCCL and WL, the opening day events represented the culmination — and celebration — of all the effort put forth up to that point. Library staff planned opening day festivities both to please and welcome patrons and to benefit the library.

## *James City County Library*

The opening of a new building presents excellent opportunities to increase community involvement with the library and expand interest among patrons in financially supporting the library. At WRL we made attempts to cash in, literally, on the excitement surrounding JCCL by creating a simple giving brochure. The brochure included named room opportunities and equipment that we wanted but could not afford. (See the brochure in Appendix D.) The pamphlet also listed any companies, organizations, and individuals who already had given their support to JCCL. The general public often does not realize that the public library is happy to accept private support and that such support can make a good library even better. The JCCL giving brochure was an effort to educate the public, and it was a good start. By opening day, the NationsBank family computer literacy center in the children's department had been furnished and equipped for $10,000; the patron computer room near the reference desk had been named and outfitted for $8,000; a small meeting room was named for $6,000; and a collection of topical books was established at $2,500.

Another exercise we planned to attract giving was a special preview of the new library for members of the Williamsburg Area Chamber of Commerce. WRL hosted what the chamber calls a Business After Hours

(BAH), a social gathering at which local business people network and relax. By holding it at JCCL before the grand opening, library staff were able to offer these community leaders a fun, private introduction to the new facility. Since WRL relies on many of these companies for ongoing support of library programs, it made sense to give them a special treat. Staff solicited in-kind donations from local businesses, including the architectural and contracting firm and some of the subcontractors, to underwrite the event. Staff served as bartenders and clean-up crews and minglers, answering questions about the new building and about the library system in general.

Opening day at JCCL was on July 7, 1996. Staff sent out hundreds of invitations to dignitaries, special library supporters, program presenters, and community leaders, as well as inviting our familiar patrons through a series of newspaper articles and announcements. An introductory ceremony of speeches by local and state government officials, large donors, and members of the library board marked the occasion. The festive atmosphere included music from a circus organ and bagpipes, the requisite cake, storytelling, showcasing of new electronic resources, and lots of appreciative patrons. It was an exciting event for everyone.

Opening days are supposed to be like that. But staff were still working on end-of-project details following opening day. Among them was limited computer equipment, the result of an oversight mentioned in an earlier chapter, and opening day collection snafus.

About two weeks before JCCL opened, the library interior was completed enough for the new materials to be shelved. The support services director and Brodart developed a delivery timetable, and shelvers and catalogers were scheduled to open the boxes and shelve the items. Working with the associated inconveniences of a construction site, the shelving crew checked off the boxes against a shipping list. They did not check individual titles against packing slips because of time constraints.

Staff discovered a number of processing mistakes as they unpacked and shelved the books. Although we did not take the time to look at each book, the shelving crew picked out a few books without labels and some labels that were wrong (for example, a book on fish had a call number for mammals; a book on contracting had a call number for vitamins; several books did not have a cutter; and some fiction labels had only the first three letters of the author's name rather than the full, spelled-out name). These items were all sent to cataloging.

The catalogers loaded the new and updated MARC records from the dozens of floppy disks sent by the vendor. It took longer than anticipated to load 35,000 records, so staff stayed through the weekend loading diskette after diskette into the four computers housed in the technical services department. We opted against having the information put on a single tape because then the library would have needed to purchase a new tape drive for the main computer to read the tape. Today the information could have been put on a CD-ROM or two, but at the time we were working with what we had.

Many of you already know what an opening day collection comprises, or at least you've gotten some idea of the enormity of the concept. An opening day collection is a major purchase that is usually part of the opening of a new or otherwise empty library, so patrons and staff won't have to look at ranges of empty shelves. Such a collection is complicated because a vendor is compressing years worth of collection development into a year or sometimes a few months. An opening day collection, for a public library anyway, is usually expensive enough that you'll have to request bids, or proposals. That means that you'll have to make up a pretty detailed bid packet to send to vendors you want to get proposals from, and also to send to vendors who request a packet. The process of soliciting or collecting bids is called RFP; the actual document or packet that is a request for proposal is also known as an RFP. Luckily, there are lots of examples of RFP packets in library land; we've included ours in Appendix B. Sometimes vendors will let you have samples they've responded to before. This is helpful, but remember they will probably give you one they've responded to successfully, so borrow from it with an appropriate sized grain of salt, and be sure to include specifications you and your staff are interested in.

The process we used began with in-person presentations by sales representatives from several vendors: two we had done business with in regular book ordering and one with wide experience in opening day collections. Based on questions we asked, previous opening day customers we spoke with, and the shiny sales brochures distributed by each vendor, we spent several weeks putting together a bid packet. We sent a copy to each of the three vendors we'd spoken with, asking them to respond by a given date. Based on their formal responses, we asked some follow-up questions and then chose a vendor. WRL did not have a county or other municipal representative on the vendor selection committee, but we did have two people who had prior experience with the bidding process. Depending on how different your budgets and selection processes are, you might consider bidding the juvenile and adult and maybe even the audiovisual materials separately.

The follow-up questions were put to the vendor's catalogers who would actually do the work, not to the sales staff alone. It was important that we be able to communicate well with the technical staff; we might also have benefited from visiting the vendors' cataloging shops.

After we chose a vendor, we received what we considered disorganized reports of title matches for all parts of the collection. It is certainly possible that library staff were not clear in describing the kinds of reports we would have found helpful. Getting a small sample report, say with ten to 20 items in each call number range, would probably have helped to see what would be easiest to work with.

Anyway, we gave the vendor a copy of our catalog database. Comparing our catalog's database to their title database, the vendor provided us a list of items they recommended for purchase. For example, if our database showed that we owned none of the titles on travel in the Caribbean that the vendor offered, the report would include those titles. As we mentioned previously, collection development and acquisitions staff took the time to compare parts of the reports to our actual catalog, and found that some of the titles recommended for purchase were already owned. Perhaps some libraries just don't check behind the vendor, or perhaps we made an error in filling out the selection profile. If you're happy with the purchase recommendations, great. Edit the quantities as needed and send the forms back. We filled out a great many order forms by hand, or attached reviews that we were currently ordering from.

The vendor purchased the items it could, and processed them according to the cataloging and processing manuals we'd sent to the vendor. Most of the materials were cataloged as directed and stored in call number order. Some vendors have huge warehouses with what amount to miniature libraries shelved therein. When you've spent all your collections budget, the vendor boxes up your opening day collection in call number order and labels each box with a packing slip so you'll know where in the stacks to open it. Then you hope that the carpeting gets laid and the shelving is erected before the books are delivered. The collection vendor will keep your materials longer, if needed, but you'll usually pay rent on the space they're taking up in the warehouse.

After JCCL's shelving, wall coverings, and floor coverings were ready to receive the books, we asked the vendor to arrange for delivery on a particular day, first thing in the morning. The shipment was large enough to require a whole truck, and it arrived mid-morning on the day specified. Collection services, cataloging, and circulation staff unpacked the books and organized them onto carts for shelving. The head of collection services determined where best to start and how much space to leave for each Dewey range, based on how many books were in each box, and we shelved in a steady parade of book carts. The catalogers' next task was to make sure the database load we received matched the books on the shelves.

In a database of 35,000, we realized we couldn't expect the vendor to get everything right. Some barcodes entered in the 949 fields had typographical errors. These items had to be tracked down and their correct barcodes entered. For the incorrect barcodes we might have missed, we devised an alternate system that we hoped would ensure they got fixed. Any item not previously corrected would be returned to cataloging after a patron checked it out for the first time. All this required was an error message to alert check-out staff that the barcode was not in the system. Staff created a "fast-add" record (some systems call them "on-the-fly") and the item went home with the patron. When the item was returned, a check-in note alerted staff to send it to cataloging.

Several categories of items had problems. Although the catalogers had specified that the bibliographic records and processing of board books were different from picture books, our vendor didn't understand; so all the new board books were processed the same way as the new picture books. WRL does not put labels on board books, but this information had not made it to our vendor's processors, so they had methodically labeled each board book. WRL staff removed all those labels so the shelvers would not be confused about where to shelve the board books. All the children's read-along cassette books had to be corrected because barcodes had been affixed separately to all the books and the cassettes, rather than one barcode on the bag that contained each set. Without reviewing each item, there was no way of telling which barcode was in the computer for the combination. It was less time consuming simply to use new barcodes and remove the vendor-supplied ones.

Mass-market paperbacks also had problems, many of which were caused by unclear communications between the catalogers at WRL and the vendor. Well into the project, WRL staff decided to have these items processed and cataloged. WRL staff had sent detailed written and illustrated instructions about how to process other items, but gave cataloging instructions for the mass-market paperbacks over the telephone. When library catalogers reviewed the records, they realized they had been unclear about what items in the bibliographic record were to be entered entirely in capital letters. The vendor's catalogers also had added the note "Imprint varies" to all mass-market paperback records rather than only to the ones where the imprint indeed varied. In the end, library staff decided it was not worth the time or money to correct these errors, since the authors, titles, and call numbers were accurate. We learned from this experience to always stick to the "put it in writing" rule.

Another error occurred in the records for dozens of western fiction books. They had the collection code *W* even though we had not specified a separate collection for westerns. The labels on the western books were the correct *F* call number with a western genre sticker, but the call numbers in the database were *W*. In addition, all the audiobooks had the genre designation missing from the holdings screen. And, despite efforts to avoid duplicate records, our catalogers found many new bibliographic records added when an old record was already in our system.

The catalogers documented all the problems they could find and forwarded them to our vendor. The vendor provided corrected records and processing in a timely manner, and adjusted our fees accordingly. Two years later, catalogers are still finding a problem now and then, but overall we estimate an error rate of not much more than 5%. Because there was neither time nor obsession-compulsion enough to go through each and every record, and look at the labels on each and every item, many mistakes passed through unnoticed.

Today, shelvers who realize they are about to shelve an item amid unrelated books continue to send four or five such items a month to the catalogers for call number checks. Most of these labels have typographical errors both on the bibliographic records and on the call number labels.

It is doubtful that errors similar to the ones we found would have been avoided with a different vendor. Creating a new collection to be integrated into a pre-existing electronic catalog and processed using a specific system is obviously a complicated process.

Having said that, there are several actions we would recommend if we had to create another opening day collection. The next time we would request examples of selection lists from the vendor(s) and specify how the lists should be organized. We would agree on a reasonable time line for the entire process, ordering as well as pulling items from the existing collections, and request regular updates on the order status of our selections. We would pay particular attention to duplicate serial subscriptions (for example, travel directories) and other standing orders, and decide well in advance what would be shelved where. While perusing the existing collections, we would rely more on printed shelf lists and less on time-consuming combing through the stacks.

The majority of the acquisitions problems and cataloging discrepancies were cleared up in the year after JCCL opened. Surprisingly, one of the biggest problems we encountered in acquisitions was the change of address. When the new library opened, the whole technical services department, including receiving, moved from WL to JCCL, which had a different mailing address. The acquisitions staff made thousands of change-of-address postcards and mailed them to all of our business contacts. After three years at JCCL, we still receive mail at the old WL address. Mail doesn't sound like a big deal, but all the other postal customers in the JCCL zip code are residential or low-volume businesses. Even though many of our book and supply orders come through private carriers, the mail carrier had to get used to delivering three and sometimes four tubs of mail per day to the library. And she didn't like it. After several months of negotiations, the library and the post office came to an agreement, thanks largely to the courtesy and helpfulness of the library's courier.

Some of the lingering mail problems were caused by changes in our standing-order plans. One of the most peculiar problems was the refusal by some publishers to consolidate accounts and renewal dates when we wanted to add extra copies of a title to an existing standing order plan. One company had us listed with three separate accounts and two mailing addresses. Most of these problems have been resolved by now, after numerous phone calls and letters. Given this experience, our acquisitions manager recommends that libraries planning a new collection review all standing order plans as early in the process as possible; that way, subscription or address changes can be timed to coincide with the renewal dates for the standing orders.

JCCL has had other persistent difficulties. As seems common to most building projects, library or otherwise, the HVAC environmental system has been troublesome from the start. Perhaps one reason for this is that different components of large HVAC systems are usually manufactured and even supplied by different vendors. For example, the thermostat and temperature sensors might be available from one vendor, while the blower comes from another vendor. Evidently this is standard operating procedure in the building world, but it seems akin to buying a car's chassis from one dealership and its brakes from another, then wondering why it spends so much time in the repair shop. Anyway, temperature control has been finicky at JCCL, with the air conditioning failing more than once. The system also is quite loud in some areas and vibrates noticeably. The hot water pipe sometimes sounds as if there's a kitten stuck in the Sheetrock. Other sounds are more like a wolf howling or a ghost moaning. As occupants of buildings in any industry can probably attest, however, HVAC systems are complicated and rarely please everyone.

Adding a new facility to a library system provides a constant stream of learning opportunities for all involved. As staff began work during the design stages, we quickly realized that reading floor plans was not an inborn skill for most of us, but we learned, more or less successfully. We also learned how interconnected spatially library services are — an excellent idea for change in one area might require unacceptable changes in another. And we learned that being prepared for unknown contingencies is essential, since construction doesn't follow one predictable linear path from start to finish. (Even if library people, architects, engineers, suppliers and construction workers were completely predictable, mother nature is going to be fickle.)

In planning staffing for JCCL, we were acutely aware that we had an existing library renowned in the community for its excellent service, and that anything less at JCCL was likely to cause dissatisfaction among our community of demanding, but also very supportive, patrons. We knew we needed to get new staff on board at least a few months ahead of JCCL's opening to get them trained, and our funders graciously agreed to that. Next we considered long-term strategies for operating two "sister" libraries that would offer the same level of service. We came up with an innovative plan that drew a chorus of "It won't work" when our director asked for reactions to it at a regional meeting of her peers. The idea fared better with WRL staff, most of whom had never worked in multi-branch locations and therefore had no preconceived notions of how they should operate. The idea was not to have a WL staff and a JCCL staff, but rather to have a WRL staff that rotated from building to building on schedules worked out in the departments. This meant that there was one youth services staff, for example, with one youth services director who supervised them all. With the addition of JCCL, the WRL youth services staff grew by 50%, so this was a scheduling and logistical challenge for everyone involved, but the department directors were the ones who would take on the brunt of the additional work. They would have many more people to be responsible for, from hiring to scheduling to evaluating. And they would be doing all that for staff in two buildings. The perceived advantages were that we would have staff trained the same way, in the same procedures for both buildings, and therefore that expectations and quality of service would be identical; we would have a staff committed to the entire library system, not primarily to one building or another, and therefore avoid the competition between branches that can sometimes develop at multi-facility systems; and that patrons used to the staff at WL would become more comfortable with JCCL faster because they would be familiar with some of the faces from the Williamsburg Library. (During the renovation of WL, of course, rotating out of the construction zone was an added benefit.) It's a source of quiet amusement among staff that some patrons still don't know we rotate; when a patron at JCCL tells a circulation assistant how much friendlier everyone is than at "the other library," we listen with great interest.

Three and a half years later, the rotating system is still in use, and although there are frustrations involved with it — taking paperwork and supplies between buildings, particularly for children's staff, tops the list.

However, youth services staff recently discussed the rotation system, and said they would not want to change to a stay-in-one-building-all-the-time system. Their big concern: they like being one staff, and think the advantages to that far outweigh the logistical complications of working in two buildings. Youth services has opted to work its night and weekend shifts at one building, and its day shifts at the other building, with two teams swapping what amounts to a home building each month. The youth services staff's conclusion about rotation's success echoes what other departments think.

Being a part of one big staff also helped in settling into a new building. Although most departments had several months to train new staff before JCCL opened, veteran staff were almost as much in the dark at the new building as new staff. Reference staff, for example, faced not only new locations for familiar items, but different collection makeups (some books were available only at WL, while others were at JCCL), a new telephone system, a public computer room, and new electronic reference materials required everyone's attention. In addition, new policies and procedures demanded refinement and development every day. Initially the two reference teams traded buildings weekly. The rotation was modified to every other week to provide reference staff with sufficient time to become familiar and comfortable with the JCCL resources. That did not last, however, since the adult collections, particularly the reference works, are quite different between buildings. The librarians concluded that spending two weeks away from either would be counterproductive. They returned to the one week rotation, which continues to the present.

Circulation staff established the *Book of Changes*, a looseleaf notebook of printed e-mail, memos of procedural changes, and whatever else might make it easier to remember what was new or different. Circulation staff rotates on a more flexible but less predictable weekly schedule than reference staff.

## *Williamsburg Library*

To thank our donors, our long-term volunteers, and special Friends, we planned an elegant thank-you party funded by the companies that renovated the library. Staff sent solicitations to the vendors, contractors, subcontractors, and other companies that played a significant role in the creation of the expanded library. With follow up calls and hard work, more than $3,300 was raised to fund this special event. In return for giving, WRL gave these companies recognition on all the invitations and nametags and on posters displayed during the event.

We invited nearly 400 donors to the Thank You Gala. Those who attended were not disappointed. Served were some of the finest desserts available, champagne, sparkling cider, and hot beverages. In addition to recognizing gala sponsors with posters, we also had posters to thank the larger library donors and to define giving opportunities. The dress and decorations were polished, and guests had a unique opportunity to enjoy the building in a private setting.

Because the Thank You Gala took place the night before the grand re-dedication of WL, leftover desserts were added to the spread of cakes available to patrons the following day. By the end of the public grand opening, all the cakes and desserts were finished.

Before the new addition at the Williamsburg Library opened to the public, the library's staff development committee offered a day of tours for employees. Those who worked primarily at JCCL or who had not been involved in moving into the new space got an in-depth look at the circulation, reference, and administrative areas, learned how each was designed and how each would function. The tour concluded with a little celebratory champagne in the director's office. A few days later, minus the champagne, the public joined us.

As with JCCL, a fun opening day celebration was the culmination of all the work. While the previous evening's gala was by invitation only, the grand opening was for the entire community. And many of them attended. Again the requisite speeches were made prior to a ribbon cutting ceremony. Then patrons explored the expanded library facility while enjoying cakes, desserts, and musical programs. Staff offered a special adopt-a-book opportunity to commemorate the grand opening. (We have an on-going adopt-a-book effort that allows patrons to fill out a form and give an expensive title or extra bestseller copy in honor or memory of someone. The donor or the honoree has the option of being first on the reserve list for the item or copy.) We also gave away scratch pads and magnets. Fresh bouquets donated by local florists gave each service desk an additional something special. It was another enjoyable opening for the system.

Of course, the next day there were more realities of the building to deal with. As with JCCL, WL had its share of problems, not the least of which was parking. Parking at WL had been a problem for years before the renovation. Parking continued to be a significant concern during the construction project and for many months following the rededication ceremony. Although WL opened on April 26, 1998, there was construction around the building for a year afterward. The City of Williamsburg combined the WL renovation project with a complete rejuvenation of the space where the main library parking lot had been located, which made for parking hassles that did not end until May 1, 1999.

The results are attractive, if not what the WRL staff and board lobbied for. What was convenient library parking is now a large grassy plaza, complete with a building-sized steel flower trellis and two water features. The library board had endorsed the original underground parking plan. There is still some parking near the building, but most of it is now located across the street in a two story terrace about 1,000 feet from the library. That provides plenty of convenient parking for most people, but we are still concerned about patrons who have difficulty walking and people with small children having to cross a busy street to get to the library. However, patron complaints about parking have virtually stopped, so we're grateful for that.

There were some things we would have liked to do but were hampered by the original architecture; for example, the lift we had in the library could only accommodate book carts. When the building was renovated, the architect made the elevator people-safe, but left it in the same shaft as the old lift. Consequently, the door is not a standard sliding elevator door, but a regular office-sized door. Patrons must seek out a staff member to operate the elevator with a key. This is inconvenient for people with small children and those who have trouble walking. The architect did not explain this complication during the design phase. There are patrons who simply do not go upstairs because they do not want to have to ask for assistance.

A number of complications resulted from the fact that WL was a renovation and not a new building. Among them is the number of public entrances WL has. At JCCL, we designed a building with one public entrance. When it first opened in 1973, WL had two entrances at opposite ends of the building, plus an entrance to the arts center theatre. As you might imagine, this plethora of exits made for challenging security and service issues. However, with parking available on all sides of the building, it made sense that patrons would not want to walk all around the structure to get inside a single entrance. The renovated building called for a new main entrance on the arts center side of the library, and staff hoped to delete the far entrance and leave only a few street parking spaces on the far side of the building. But, for primarily political reasons, we still have all three entrances.

Another renovation related problem is that one of the book drop closets is now located in a public area. The door needs to be locked at all times, an inconvenience check-in staff would have been happy not to have. There have also been continuing roof leaks from the old part of the building that were supposed to be fixed during the renovation but were not. We discovered after the fact that one of the leaks is the result of a skylight that was covered instead of being removed during the construction process. Who would have guessed we needed to be on the roof as well as in the building watching for such details?

Another small problem after the renovation included keys not working in locks. (The locks at WL were specified to match those at JCCL, so staff would only have to carry one key.) For a few months staff could not unlock one of the entrances from the outside of WL because the locking mechanism was not properly aligned with the door frame. Two catalog terminals that were supposed to be in the fiction stacks were eliminated because the conduit that was supposed to house the data connections was never installed during the renovation.

On the whole, both JCCL and WL turned out well. Most of the continuing problems are more nuisances that can be handled with a quiet complaint or even an ironic chuckle, and can often be fixed. With the construction projects behind us, we can look back and simultaneously wonder how we survived and be grateful for the buildings we now have. We hope we've been clear that during a library construction project there is as much a role for library staff as there is for the people building the library. If library staff ignore their place in the construction process, they will likely regret the results.

# Appendix A:
# Construction Timeline

This construction project timeline spans seventeen years, from the first concept that we might need a second library building through the end of the renovations at WL. Most of those years were spent waiting or planning. It took as long to obtain funding for the construction projects as it did to actually build everything.

---

## *1981*

- James City County (JCC) Long Range Plan mentions need for library in James City County.

## *1989*

- City of Williamsburg and JCC hire Carol Brown Associates to do long-range facilities feasibility study.

## *1990*

JUNE

- WL closes on Fridays to use library space more efficiently (slow patron day, so staff can use public study areas to do collection development and other off-desk tasks).

NOVEMBER

- Carol Brown issues report calling for central library in the Norge/Light-foot area; 20,000 square foot branch in Kingsmill area; expansion of Williamsburg Library "immediately." Branches in Stonehouse, Rt. 5, and Grove to follow. (Norge [JCCL] and Williamsburg happen).

## 1991

- JCC establishes committee to search for land for Upper County library. Committee members look at parcels from the New Town area, through the Olde Towne area to the Lightfoot/Toano corridor. No recommendations are made.
- Letters from Kristiansand Homeowners Association and Bruce Keener saying the library should go in the Norge/Toano area, not the Olde Towne area, when Olde Towne is reported in the paper as a possible location.
- JCC capital budget assumptions show: FY94—$3,000,000 GO bonds—Library; FY95—$2,400,000 GO bonds—Library.

## 1992

- Expansion of WL is highest priority of Williamsburg Planning Commission.
- Tenth anniversary celebration of opening of the arts center and youth services wing of WL.
- Information sent to JCC Administrator David Norman recommending 1.0 square feet per capita as goal for JCCL, instead of state "guideline" of .6 square feet per capita.
- Bids received to repair WL roof—$140,000.

## 1993

FEBRUARY

- The Design Collaborative is hired to do feasibility study to determine how much the Williamsburg Library can comfortably be expanded, and how much space will be needed for a library in the Norge area.

MARCH

- New contract for library services between city and county: The Williamsburg Library will remain the "administrative center" for the regional library system. JCC will build a second library building; Williamsburg will expand and renovate the existing library.

MAY

- Library director appointed to JCC referendum advisory group.
- JCCL site selection committee meets— library director, Murden (Trustee), Lysaght (Trustee), and JCC staff from finance and planning.

AUGUST

- Site selection committee reports to JCC Board of Supervisors (BOS) that the Norge/Lightfoot area is best location for JCCL.

SEPTEMBER

- Architect Ed Lazaron reports on feasibility study for JCCL to library board and to JCC BOS. Some supervisors think the project too large — the public will not vote for anything over 25,000 square feet.

OCTOBER

- Library board endorses 34,000 square foot new library, and $6.1 million for library part of bond referendum.

NOVEMBER

- Referendum set for March 1, 1994.

## *1994*

JANUARY

- Lazaron presents WL feasibility plan — possibility of closing Scotland Street entrance becomes an issue.

FEBRUARY

- Bond referendum heats up. Lazaron does designs to take to meetings.

Friends of WRL print and distribute referendum pins. Library director attends meetings of many community groups to sell the library part of the referendum. Lee Scruggs is most effective member of citizen group lobbying for the library part of the referendum.

## MARCH

- Library gets 78.1 percent of the referendum vote — a "landside" according to the paper.

## APRIL

- Planning for staffing begins. Library director suggests two libraries operated with same public service departments but public service staff rotating between buildings.

## JULY

- Meeting at Norge Community Hall for citizen input into JCCL plans. Community generally likes the plans, but prefers preserving more trees. Architect returns to drawing board and does plan to preserve more trees.

## OCTOBER–NOVEMBER

- Staff visits other libraries — Manassas, Chinn Park, Chesapeake, Chapel Hill, Fayetteville, Fredericksburg, etc.

## DECEMBER

- Hopke and Associates hired to design WL expansion and renovation.

# 1995

## JANUARY

- Scotland Street entrance closing controversy heats up.

## MARCH

- Letter from Murden about WL construction budget. Letter from Tuttle (City Manager) saying $2,547,000 is absolutely the limit.
- Bids open for JCCL — first project in area in years to come in under budget.
- Plans to open JCCL with 70,000 volumes, half new, half recycled and to double in 5 to 10 years. (In November 1999 it had 116,915.)

APRIL

- Hopke presents first "concept" design, which trustees approve; includes curved walls.
- JCCL groundbreaking.

JUNE

- Search for JCCL Opening Day vendor starts—$680,000 initial budget.
- Board and staff give in rather than have a city council vote—Scotland Street entrance will remain open, as "main entrance" to the library.

AUGUST

- Master Gardeners, under the leadership of Mary Ann Brendel, receive $4,500 grant for children's garden at JCCL.

SEPTEMBER

- Circulation department splits into check-in and check-out.
- First look at Northington Block design—includes drive around at library; small water feature.
- Photo in *Virginia Gazette*—Steel going up at "library in Norge" (JCCL).

OCTOBER

- Williamsburg Architectural Review Board approves WL plan without curved walls.

NOVEMBER

- Support services director reports to the board on plans for building the JCCL collection.
- Giving Brochure for JCCL is distributed.
- Report from Madeleine Conway, JCC total quality performance analyst, says JCCL staffing request is "appropriate," although more management staff may be needed in the future.

## *1996*

JANUARY

- Snow interrupts construction at JCCL—temporary structure constructed to keep it warm enough to do masonry work.

- BOS approves spring hiring for JCCL new positions.
- Start of construction at WL postponed two months as Northington Block (block on which WL is located) plans are still being developed (turn around drive still under discussion).

## FEBRUARY

- Letter from library board to planning commission and city council asking to keep drop-off point and handicapped parking convenient to parking lot entrance at WL.
- Library director meets with JCC Planning Commission questioning inclusion of "library" in New Town plans. Library director replies that neither the library staff nor the trustees were consulted about the plans, and that the library's long range plan calls for the next library to be constructed in the Rt. 5 area.
- Staff begins streamlining meetings, etc., to leave as much time as possible for organizing opening day collection, equipment purchases and automation configurations, advertising, filling, planning for training for new positions.
- Begin study of providing Internet access for the public.

## MARCH

- Decision is made to open JCCL without recorded music collection.
- 180 boxes of Pit books have been packed for JCCL.
- Letters to contractors, architects, etc., asking for help with Business After Hours (a monthly Chamber of Commerce function for local business leaders to meet in an informal setting) at JCCL.
- Library director and county construction manager Farmer get JCC award for bringing JCCL in below budget.
- *Virginia Gazette* says: "City Parking May go Under Ground."
- "New and Notable" winning entry for new books area at JCCL.
- JCCL telephones being set up through JCC.

## APRIL

- May 20–22 target for furniture installation at JCCL.
- WL interior plan almost complete — staff involved in planning furnishings.
- Hiring proceeds for JCCL, also equipment and supplies purchasing.

## May

- Budget approved by JCC BOS will not accommodate Friday openings at JCCL.
- JCCL Fundraising effort successes: McGaws: $8,000; Cosby, $6,000; NationsBank, $10,000; Massies, $2,500.
- Move books to JCCL: collection services in charge. Hires Kloke Moving, uses JCC staff and Cheatham Annex volunteers.
- Furniture and wiring installations at JCCL. Circulation director's connections schedule sent out by Lazaron.

## June

- Computer moved to JCCL on June 3. Four days of down time. Data line apparently installed improperly by Bell Atlantic. Collection services checks in 8,000 books in four hours when system comes up.
- *Daily Press* reports that delays in "downtown redevelopment" mean delay for start of construction at WL.
- *Virginia Gazette* editor receives special tour of JCCL, writes mostly positive editorial about same.
- Visits to JCCL from other libraries begin, first by York County library trustees, who give $200 to the JCCL fundraising effort.
- WRL leases some computers to open JCCL on time when JCC purchasing fails to get them delivered in time. WRL staff take over remainder of equipment purchases for JCCL. Move of technical services delayed a month for the same reason.

## July

- July 2 — Business After Hours at JCCL.
- July 7 — JCCL opens on schedule with 80,000 books.
- Work starts on WRL webpage.

## September

- Summer reading attendance is third highest in the state.
- Technical services moves to JCCL, two months behind schedule, due to JCC purchasing problems.

## October

- Construction bids opened for WL.

NOVEMBER

- Collection services director is working to finish interior design plans.
- Groundbreaking set for December 2.
- Departments at WL moved to TAFKATS. Off-desk work is scheduled for JCCL to free up parking downtown for patrons.

DECEMBER

- Circulation desk moves to share arts center desk.
- Project engineer Greg Dunkle moves to former circulation office.

## *1997*

JANUARY

- Letter from library board to city council expressing concern about distance from WL to handicapped parking in plaza plans.
- Internet up for public and all staff.
- JCCL — breaking-in period continues — wallpaper, reference workroom door frame, glitches in HVAC.
- January 1 — letter from Louise Hutchinson: "The [JCCL] building is a wedding of books and light that gives wings to the spirit as a library should."
- Most critical time for parking will be after construction begins on underground parking.
- JCC BOS agree to pay their part of new bookmobile with residual JCCL funds.

FEBRUARY

- City agrees to fund their part of the bookmobile.
- Temporary wall goes up at WL — steel is going up outside.
- JCCL breaking in continues: reference workroom file units being reconfigured, still waiting on parts; three replacement tables delivered — one damaged; HVAC laptop being repaired; Paralax keyboard trays installed; roof leaks fixed; youth services LED animation software delivered, training awaits.
- Visit from Virginia Beach library staff.
- Visit from N. Shelby County (Alabama) library staff.

- Letter to the editor from library director — apology for "noisy" phase of construction coming up; thanks for patience during our "growing pains."
- Six months report on JCCL to JCC BOS.

## MARCH

- Using fund balances for equipment at WL — no equipment in the budget.
- JCCL — carpet cleaning demos, still "another search for the guilty" on the shredding of the Bola upholstery. (October, 1999, ongoing, but a fix appears to be in sight).

## MAY

- WRLF sponsors fundraising workshop for North Carolina and Virginia libraries at JCCL.
- Commitment from Gladys and Franklin Clark Foundation on furniture for WL — $253,000.
- "Contract" letter from Williamsburg Garden Club about Scotland Street water feature.
- Small fire in construction area at WL.
- ETOP in effect — negotiating for portable AC unit.
- Summer Reading Plans — *Building Better Readers* incorporates construction theme, Uncle Dunkle does storytimes.

## JULY

- City council votes not to proceed with underground parking.
- Youth services director finalizes plans for Kids Book Xpress from December, 1997 to May, 1998.
- WL construction timeline developed.

## AUGUST

- *Virginia Gazette* reports Chamber of Commerce headed to Northington Block.

## SEPTEMBER

- Letter from program services director to *Virginia Gazette* on parking.
- Letter from trustees on parking.

- Library director submits plan for plaza and parking.
- City manager attends trustees meeting about parking.
- Library board votes to continue support for underground parking.
- Modular furniture from office building across street (slated for demolition) disassembled by WRL facilities staff and stored.

OCTOBER

- Trustees invite city council to meeting to discuss parking.
- WL is on schedule for adult area at WL to open January 3. Kids Book Xpress to open December 6.
- City council votes modified Northington Plan, without chamber building.
- Chair of trustees sends letter on parking to *Virginia Gazette*.

NOVEMBER

- Chair of trustees sends letter to city council following meeting — library board still thinks plaza should be moved to make room for more parking.
- Construction company informs WRL that youth services can stay open until end of February; Kids Book Xpress has to open only March–April.
- Construction for downtown parking will not begin until April, 1998, at the earliest.
- Letter from architect to those in opposition to library trustees' wishes about plaza, sent without consulting with trustees or staff.
- Planning commission approves long-range plan that includes underground parking.

## *1998*

DECEMBER–JANUARY, 97-98

- Close December 17 to January 2 to relocate new books to new adult services area; close adult nonfiction behind temporary wall; patrons can still return books, check out reserves, and use JCCL; 25 percent of adult collection available for circulation at WL.
- Business remains about 75 percent of pre-construction time at WL in spite of inconveniences associated with construction.

- Collection services director gets all the furniture we need and more within budget, and saves us $40,000 for equipment.
- Library director does presentation to Ford's Colony newcomers—90 percent have cards; 80 percent use JCCL.
- New schedule for completion of WL.
- Administration, reference, collection services and circulation move into new work spaces at WL.
- Boundary Office Building to be razed for parking terrace (building from which modular furniture came).

## FEBRUARY

- Library closes to eliminate "temporary" wall—closed off part of adult services visible to public as carpet laid, etc.
- February 23—rest of adult services collection opens; tax help in space where periodical shelving will go eventually.
- 18–22: adult books come up from the Pit; kids books go down.

## MARCH

- Human resources director has surgery—popped a disk during re-shelving.
- JCCL wins Arbor Day award.
- Kids Book Xpress opens on March 2.

## APRIL

- Library staff and project manager participate in Earl Gregg Swem Library (at College of William and Mary) staff day to help them prepare for their construction project.
- Thank You Gala for donors at WL.
- Additional costs for Scotland Street water feature will be paid by city, says city.
- Rededication celebration—chair of BOS and mayor of Williamsburg tell stories to children.
- April newsletter—rededication celebration cover letter from library director.

## MAY

- Work on plaza in front of WL begins—more parking goes.

## JUNE

- Dunkle leaves.

## JULY

- Board agrees to divide music compact disc collection between JCCL and WL.
- Meeting room use up 12.4 percent at WL in spite of construction outside — credit to program services director.
- New bookmobile goes into service.
- Start opening half-days on Fridays.

## SEPTEMBER

- Silent auction of all leftover or broken furniture and equipment.
- Old bookmobile transferred to Heritage Public Library in Providence Forge.
- *Williamsburg Homes* features WRL: "Two locations to serve you."
- Board letter asking for parking along drive around community building — eventually got six spaces.
- Water feature update: to be completed by May 1. "What the Williamsburg Garden Club is unable to fund, the city will pick up."
- Plaza, parking deck and community center all on schedule for completion by May 1.

## DECEMBER

- Parking terrace completed by January 1.
- Concerns about height of wall around Plaza letter sent to city council.
- Staff begin parking in terrace — lighting still not finished.

# Appendix B:
# Support Services RFP

The request for proposal that covered the new book collection at JCCL was carefully prepared by staff. We include it here in the hopes that it may prove a useful reference.

---

**James City County
Library Opening Day Materials Collection
Request for Proposal
95-P-0015**

## I.   BACKGROUND

The Williamsburg Regional Library system (WRL), which includes James City County, currently consists of one building and a bookmobile with a combined annual circulation of 750,000.

WRL uses Dynix circulation, acquisitions, and cataloging modules and OCLC to obtain machine-readable records for automated cataloging. WRL plans to continue using these.

Dynix version 135 on an Ultimate 3040 CPU is being used but will be changing soon; the database consists of approximately 165,000 bibliographic records.

The budget for materials for the new James City County Library is approximately $680,000 including processing charges. Money for the opening day book collection will come from special funding rather than from the book budget.

## II.  PURPOSE

This request for proposal involves the JCCL which will be constructed in Norge, Virginia. Current status for beginning construction of the new library will be within a May–June, 1995 timeframe. The anticipated opening date for the new library is July 1, 1996. Opening day books are to be delivered by June 1, 1996.

WRL will purchase approximately 35,000 volumes for JCCL over a period of 15 months. The same number of books will be transferred from the Williamsburg facility. Prior to the ordering of materials, WRL will provide automation hardware and software specifications to the successful proposer.

## III. SCOPE OF WORK

The proposal shall address Collection Development Services to include but not be limited to:

A.  How Collection Development Will Take Place

   1.  Provide customized selection lists to include inventory status, review media citation, and groupings by subject, age interest and format.

   2.  Provide a minimum of 200 sources from which selections may be made.

   3.  Include adult, young adult, juvenile, reference and large print books; videos, spoken cassettes and compact discs. A list of sources that include these titles shall be provided.

   4.  Outline how you will ensure that the bibliographies are as current as possible.

   5.  Provide a Collection Development Specialist to come to the Williamsburg location to finalize collection development planning.

B.  Creation of Selection Lists

   1.  Format of lists.

   2.  Whether JCCL may choose how the lists will be arranged and/or organized.

   3.  How the "out of print" and "must order direct" titles will be treated.

   4.  How duplicate titles among sources will be handled.

5. Options and costs for providing WRL with selection lists that combine WRL holdings and list of available (in-print) titles. The printouts should be updated every 2–3 months, be in shelf-list order and be designed so WRL staff can quickly and easily determine:

   a) the number of copies of each title currently owned per Dynix agency,

   b) mark the number of desired opening day copies,

   c) determine the number of copies already on order.

C. Placing Orders

   The proposer shall agree to accept return of materials found to be defective, not as ordered, or to credit processing charges for processing errors.

   The proposer shall list discount schedules and processing fees for each type of material: adult books, juvenile books, audio materials, video materials and other materials at the proposer's discretion.

   The proposer shall track amounts spent on adult and juvenile titles through separate accounts.

   Include a description of the options by which WRL may place orders, including marking printed lists and ordering electronically.

   1. Report items not available, regardless of ordering option.

   2. Provide option to receive alternate editions.

   3. How titles chosen from available selection lists will be handled.

   4. How titles selected by WRL that are not available will be handled.

   5. Procedures that will be made available to help WRL manage these selections.

   6. Whether WRL will be allowed to select titles using sources other than those provided and how the order will be placed.

   7. How prevention of duplicate orders will be handled without restricting ordering of multiple copies of the same title.

   8. How WRL will be assisted in specifying the latest possible editions of serial publications.

   9. At what point WRL may cancel orders for specific items.

D.   Cataloging Rules and Processing Requirements

All processing supplies unless otherwise noted shall be furnished by the proposer. Processing samples shall be approved by the library prior to start of project.

1.   Cataloging specification sheet to be submitted by library prior to onset of cataloging.

2.   Proposer will send cataloger(s) to WRL to finalize cataloging requirements.

3.   Processing specification sheet to be submitted by library prior to cataloging, detailing label location, taping, etc. Processing of books for opening day collection shall include:

    a)   attached jackets for hard cover volumes,

    b)   outside spine tape and inside spine tape for trade paperbacks,

    c)   barcodes,

    d)   spine labels,

    e)   property stamping,

    f)   security strips,

    g)   genre labels.

4.   Provide description of options and costs for online cataloging via modem in WRL catalog; proposer's loading a copy of WRL database and periodically updating WRL catalog and other machine cataloging options the vendor offers.

5.   Provide an identical classification number for any title which is already in WRL database or a revised classification number if WRL wishes.

6.   Provide description of procedures that will be followed for cataloging titles that are not in WRL database.

7.   Proposer shall be able to catalog books to the exact specifications provided by WRL.

8.   Provide the source of cataloging database and describe how you will handle cataloging for titles ordered directly from the publisher.

E.   Database Update Requirements

WRL shall have on-line access to the cataloging database, so WRL can monitor the status of the project.

1. The proposer shall provide holdings update tapes to OCLC at WRL request. These records should only be for non-duplicate titles added to the library's database during the course of the project. Any OCLC numbers thus updated must also be added to the appropriate WRL bibliographic records.

2. Explain the method and frequency by which you will handle updates of WRL database.

3. Outline what procedure will be employed, using WRL standard, to consolidate duplicate records created by WRL and the proposer during the course of the project.

F. Storage and Shipment

Stored books must be sorted into one classification sequence regardless of the number of orders being interfiled.

Materials ordered from a third source but processed by the opening day proposer shall be sorted into one classification sequence and stored together.

Proposer will price strict classification sort logic and loose classification sort logic.

1. Outline how books will be packed, labeled and stored until building is complete.

2. Outline the procedures WRL will follow when it opts to audit books in storage.

3. Outline the steps proposer will take to guarantee the security of stored books (in particular, is it proposer's insurance or WRL insurance which protects materials in storage?).

4. Proposer will explain what options it offers for inside delivery, including timing and means of shipment. JCCL will provide staff for shelving collection.

G. Project Reports

WRL and proposer will agree on fund disbursement schedule prior to ordering of materials.

1. Proposer shall outline and price types of reports available and in what frequency in order to assist WRL in monitoring titles ordered, backordered, canceled, etc. to include:

   a) processing or storage history report,

   b) title reports as requested,

c)   invoice register,

d)   monthly summary reports.

3.   Proposer shall outline and price the types and frequency of fund accounting reports that will be available. Will the proposer be able to assist in the managing and reporting on titles ordered directly from the publishers, especially on expenditures for these books?

H.   Work Plan

Proposer will appoint a liaison to provide support during all phases of project development and implementation.

WRL will provide a list of contact staff prior to onset of project, including coordinator, acquisitions contact, cataloging contact, collection development contact and automation contact.

Proposer shall outline its resources currently in place that will ensure that the requirements can be met on schedule to include:

1.   a recommended project schedule.

2.   an outline of in-progress or completed projects that are similar in nature to this request to include amount of contract, number of books involved, service provided, and the name, address and phone number of a contact person.

3.   submit at least three specific public library references for which the company has performed the same or similar services in the past two years.

4.   list the company staff who will make up the project team, including their qualifications and whether and for how long they have worked on similar projects.

5.   provide cost saving suggestions that do not negatively affect quality.

I.   Invoicing

1.   Proposer will indicate cataloging and processing charges on invoice for materials extended by line item.

2.   Invoices will be submitted in quadruplicate.

3.   Invoice will show for each title the number of copies, title, author, publisher, unit list price rate of discount, net unit price and extended net amount.

4.   Proposer will indicate purchase order number on all shipping documents and invoices.

## IV.  EVALUATION PROCEDURES

Evaluation will be based on the criteria set forth below on a scale of 1–5:

| Factor | | Weight |
|---|---|---|
| A. | Approach, work plan and price | 25 |
| B. | Management plan and timetable | 25 |
| C. | Project team qualifications and Experience | 25 |
| D. | Firm experience and capabilities | 25 |

April 27, 1995

TO:       RFP 95-P-0015 Vendors
FROM:   Serena Paisley, Support Services Director
SUBJECT:  Clarification of RFP

This amendment to RFP 95-P-0015 is in response to questions posed by several vendors. I have tried to answer them in the order of the original document.

## I.  BACKGROUND

The Dynix 14X system is to be installed in June and will limit system access for approximately 2–3 days. We will also be loading the 150 upgrade in September or October with similar downtime.

The materials budget breaks down by the following approximate percentages and amounts. We have reserved $80,000 for direct orders.

| | | | |
|---|---|---|---|
| Books: | | 87% | $522,000 |
| | Adult | 60% | 313,200 |
| | Juvenile | 40% | 208,800 |
| Audio: | | 5% | $30,000 |
| | Adult | 60% | 18,000 |
| | CD | 20% | 3,600 |
| | Books on tape | 80% | 14,400 |
| | Juvenile | 40% | 12,000 |
| Videos: | | 8% | $48,000 |
| | Adult | 60% | 28,800 |
| | Feature | 60% | 17,280 |
| | Non-feature | 40% | 11,520 |
| | Juvenile | 40% | 19,200 |

III.    SCOPE OF WORK

A-2: The 200 sources would include review sources and recommended lists for all media.

A-3: "Sources" refers to review sources.

B-2: Selection lists should be customized. The obvious arrangement would be by type of media, then by collection category (i.e. adult fiction, juvenile nonfiction), then by call number. We would like the flexibility to change the sorting of these lists to a title or author or call number arrangement if needed.

B-3: We would like for out-of-print titles to be left off of lists. Direct order titles should be included by clearly identified.

B-5: Nine-track tapes are not used by our new system. It uses DAT tape cassettes which we assume can hold our current collection by holding agency.

C-5: This may be a summary statement concerning C-1 through C-4, i.e., an outline of order management procedures.

D.   Cataloging and processing:

Cataloging:

WRL would require Library of Congress CIP records to be fully upgraded. Mass market paperbacks are cataloged only in Dynix.

WRL does not follow standard Dewey classification in some of the following areas:

law
Virginia genealogy
literature (cutters only)
artists (cutters only)
biography
fiction
easy (picture books)
easy readers
juvenile collected biography
juvenile Native Americans
juvenile geography

Processing:

We use the following genre labels which do not include the collection designations such as ESL, ABE, M (adult mystery) which head up the call number on the spine label or color-coding dots which separate out juvenile concept books and adult paperbacks. Approximately 2 percent of the adult books and 8 percent of the juvenile books need these labels:

Adult
  Fantasy
  Westerns

Juvenile
  Easy reader
  Horses
  Mystery
  Science fiction
  Young adult

Adult and juvenile paperbacks
  Fantasy
  Mystery
  Science Fiction

Other processing specifications include:

  1 barcode
  3M security strip
  2 property stamps
  1 date received stamp
  1 spine label
  reference labels
  video/cd/audio special labels
  reinforcing of quality paperbacks
  taped plastic book jacket covers
  1 county library identification dot

D-6:We expect 10 percent or less of ordered titles to be new to our database.

E.  Database Update
    Samples of Dynix holding record information attached.

F.  Storage and shipment
    Third source materials are to be interfiled with the rest of the collection.

    F-7: The building is accessible by tractor-trailer, has no loading dock and no stairs.

G-1:All of these reports are for tracking progress. We would like to have reports of how many and what titles have been processed, i.e., completed. We would need these to verify our invoices, also.

G-3:See I. Background.

I hope these answers will help you formulate a more accurate bid.

# Appendix C:
# Computer Workstation Specs

Before seeking bids for equipment purchases, WRL's automated services department developed minimum equipment specifications for each type of workstation we would be ordering. This process helped us define the types of use to take place at each workstation and better map work flow. It also proved invaluable in comparing widely varying bids on such items as PCs and printers to determine which bid gave us the best value on equipment that would meet our needs. While the 1997 specifications are outdated in their particulars, they can serve as a model for defining workstation needs.

---

Williamsburg Regional Library
Automated Services
8/97 JF

## Basic PC Workstation
## Specifications

Workstations ordered for basic staff office use should meet the following *minimum* specifications.

- Pentium 166 processor
- 32 MB EDO RAM
- 1.6 GB hard drive
- 2 MB video RAM
- 3Comm Etherlink II 10base T network card

- 3.5" floppy disk drive
- 12x CD-ROM drive
- 3 PCI slots
- 3 ISA slots
- 4 peripheral bays
- 2 serial/1 parallel ports
- PCI local bus video & IDE disk controller
- MS ergonomic mouse
- tower case
- Win95 keyboard
- 14" SVGA monitor (.28 dp)
- loaded with Windows 95

To be ordered with each workstation:

- Corel WordPerfect Suite 7
- Norton AntiVirus
- mouse pad

## CD Workstation
## Specifications

Workstations ordered for use of CD-ROM programs by the public in adult and youth services areas should meet the following *minimum* specifications.

- Pentium 166 processor
- 32 MB EDO RAM
- 1.6 GB hard drive
- 2 MB video RAM
- 3Comm Etherlink II 10base T network card
- 3.5" floppy disk drive
- multi-disk CD-ROM changer (minimum of 4)
- 3 PCI slots
- 3 ISA slots
- 4 peripheral bays
- 2 serial/1 parallel ports

- PCI local bus video & IDE disk controller
- 16 bit sound card & set of speakers
- MS ergonomic mouse
- tower case
- Win95 keyboard
- 14" SVGA monitor (.28 dp)
- loaded with Windows 95

To be ordered with each workstation:

- Norton AntiVirus
- (security software)
- mouse pad

## Internet PC Workstation Specifications

Workstations for use by patrons to access the library's automated system card catalog, library network, and the internet should meet the following *minimum* specifications.

- Pentium 166 processor
- 32 MB EDO RAM
- 1.6 GB hard drive
- 2 MB video RAM
- 3Comm Etherlink II 10base T network card
- 3.5" floppy disk drive
- 12x CD-ROM drive
- 3 PCI slots
- 3 ISA slots
- 4 peripheral bays
- 2 serial/1 parallel ports
- PCI local bus video & IDE disk controller
- MS ergonomic mouse
- tower case
- Win95 keyboard
- 14" SVGA monitor (.28 dp)
- loaded with Windows 95

To be ordered with each workstation:

- Norton AntiVirus
- (security software)
- System Commander
- mouse pad

## Notebook PC Workstation
## Specifications

Workstations for use by staff at off-site locations to access the library's automated system, library network and the Internet from the library bookmobile & to perform basic office tasks while traveling should meet the following *minimum* specifications.

- Pentium 133 processor
- 16 MB EDO RAM
- 1.6 GB hard drive
- integrated 3.5" floppy disk drive
- integrated 8x CD-ROM drive
- 2 Type III PCMCIA slots
- 1 serial/1 parallel port
- 12" active-matrix color display
- 33.6 internal modem or PCMCIA modem card
- 3Comm Etherlink III 10BT ethernet PC card
- loaded with Windows 95

To be ordered with each workstation:

- Norton AntiVirus
- Corel Suite 7

## Public Service Desk Terminal
## Specifications

Workstations for use by staff at public service desk locations where access to the library's automated system is the only requirement should meet the following *minimum* specifications.

- 14" flat screen with display area of 26 lines x 80 columns
- green phosphor display
- US ASCII keyboard
- support for full duplex, 8 data bits, 1 stop bit, XON/XOFF & DTR handshake protocols, odd, even or none parity, 9600 baud rate
- 2 RS-232 serial ports & 1 parallel port
- built-in screen-saving mode
- 12 programmable function keys, holding characters each

## Basic Workstation Printer Specifications

Printer for use by staff with Basic PC Workstations for printing text and graphics in either black or color on varied paper sizes should meet the following *minimum* specifications.

- inkjet printer capable of 600x600 dpi black output and 600x300 dpi color output
- 8 ppm black and 4 ppm color
- ethernet network connectivity
- capable of printing on a variety of paper sizes, including banners
- automatic sheet paper feeding of more than 50 pages
- compatible with Win95

## Public Area Printer Specifications

Printer for use by patrons with public service desk terminals, Internet PC workstations, CD workstations, and literacy center workstations in the public areas of the library to print directly from terminals to printer should meet the following *minimum* specifications. Each printer will be shared by two or more terminals.

- inkjet printer capable of 600x300 dpi black output
- compact size
- automatic sheet feeding of at least 50 pages
- compatible with Win95

# Appendix D:
# Fundraising Materials

Fundraising and construction can go hand in hand. Here are some examples of fundraising materials that came together during the construction and renovation at Williamsburg Regional Library. Included are small versions of posters we created for the gala to thank donors the night before WL was rededicated and the invitation we sent to donors. Also there is a reproduction of our Perpetual Book Fund brochure and a giving list produced in conjunction with the completion of JCCL.

The Williamsburg Regional Library Foundation board
thanks the following donors for their tremendous
commitments to the library


Anheuser-Busch, Inc.
Anonymous
John and Scottie Austin
William J. Bennett
Brodart Company
Corydon B. Butler, Jr.
J. Genelle Caldwell
Gladys and Franklin Clark Foundation
Isabelle B. Cosby
College and University Computers
Friedman Family
Friends of the Williamsburg Regional Library
James J. Govern & Patsy J. Hansel
Governor's Land at Two Rivers
Helen Lee
Jack L. Massie Contractors, Inc.
Jane G. and Robert McGaw
James City County/Williamsburg Master Gardeners Assoc.
NationsBank
Schell Family
Carol and Roger Sherman
Robert B. Sigafoes
Williamsburg Garden Club
Williamsburg Junior Woman's Club
Widomaker Communication Services, Inc.


In Memory of
Lee Peltier, Sr.
Barbara L. and Joseph L. Serrill

# THANK YOU FOR THE

READING ROOM FURNISHINGS
BY THE GLADYS I. AND FRANKLIN W. CLARK FOUNDATION

GARDEN WATER FEATURE
BY THE WILLIAMSBURG GARDEN CLUB

PATRICIA SCHELL MEMORIAL MEETING ROOM
BY THE SCHELL FAMILY

FAMILY COMPUTER LITERACY CENTER
BY JANE G. AND ROBERT MCGAW

CHILDREN'S BOOK ART COLLECTION IN MEMORY OF SUSANNE
AUSTIN
BY HELEN LEE

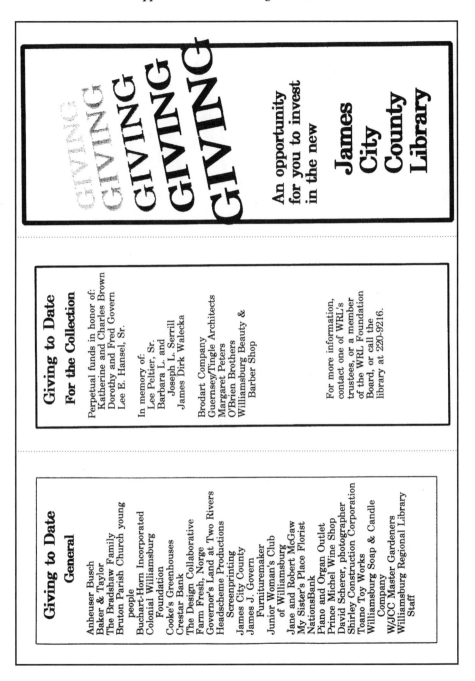

## GIVING GIVING GIVING GIVING GIVING GIVING

An opportunity for you to invest in the new

**James City County Library**

### Giving to Date
#### For the Collection

Perpetual funds in honor of:
Katherine and Charles Brown
Dorothy and Fred Govern
Lee E. Hansel, Sr.

In memory of:
Lee Peltier, Sr.
Barbara L. and
Joseph L. Serrill
James Dirk Walecka

Brodart Company
Guernsey/Tingle Architects
Margaret Peters
O'Brien Brothers
Williamsburg Beauty &
Barber Shop

For more information, contact one of WRL's trustees, or a member of the WRL Foundation Board, or call the library at 220-9216.

### Giving to Date
#### General

Anheuser Busch
Baker & Taylor
The Bradshaw Family
Bruton Parish Church young
people
Buchart-Horn Incorporated
Colonial Williamsburg
Foundation
Cooke's Greenhouses
Crestar Bank
The Design Collaborative
Farm Fresh, Norge
Governor's Land at Two Rivers
Headscheme Productions
Screenprinting
James City County
James J. Govern
Furnituremaker
Junior Woman's Club
of Williamsburg
Jane and Robert McGaw
My Sister's Place Florist
NationsBank
Piano and Organ Outlet
Prince Michel Wine Shop
David Scherer, photographer
Shirley Construction Corporation
Toano Toy Works
Williamsburg Soap & Candle
Company
W/JCC Master Gardeners
Williamsburg Regional Library
Staff

Welcome to the James City County Library.

JCCL plus the library in Williamsburg comprise the Williamsburg Regional Library system. The Williamsburg Library is one of the busiest in Virginia, and we believe that JCCL will be equally as successful.

James City County citizens made the James City County Library possible by overwhelmingly voting for bond funding for the library on March 1, 1994. Private donations are helping to make the library even better.

Any member of the WRL Board of Trustees or Foundation Board will be happy to discuss giving opportunities with you.

*Linda Gardner Massie*
Linda Gardner Massie, Chairman
WRL Board of Trustees

Marty Jones
Nancy V. Archibald
Ken Wolfe
Pat Curd
I. Trotter Hardy
Ursula Murden
Mary Ann Brendel

*Sarah Houghland*
Sarah Houghland, Chairman
WRL Foundation Board

Herbert Bell
Linda Caviness
Connie Granger
George Healy
Jayne Allen
Betty Parkany
Deborah Vick
Linda Gardner Massie
Joseph N. Rountree

## For the Collection

**Perpetual book fund.** Purchase at least one book a year in perpetuity. . . . . **minimum $500**

**Purchase a core collection** of reference materials in a particular area of information (e.g., business, art, computers, medicine). . . . . **$1,000-$3,000**

**Named collection** of books, magazines, books-on-tape or videos. . . . . **$5,000-$25,000**

**Special book purchases.** A classic title, best seller, book-on-tape, or video . . . . . **minimum $25**

## Special Items

**Storytelling Pavilion** to be located in the Children's Arboretum, designed by the Williamsburg/JCC Master Gardeners. . . . . **$60,000**

**Garden statuary, or a water feature, or special plantings** in the Arboretum. . . . . **$500-$7,500**

**Video projector** for the public meeting room. . . . . **$7,500**

**Videotape checker** . . . . . **$7,500**

**Camcorder** for recording programs and staff training activities . . . . . **$1,500**

**Group study room** . . . . . **$5,000**

**Community Room** for programs and meetings . . . . . **$35,000**

## Technology

**Computer, printer and software** for a business information resource station. . . . . **$5,000**

**Online periodical data base** will enable library users to do research in magazines online, some even before they are published in hard copy. . . . **$30,000**

**Public computer terminal** . . . **$2,500**

**Public computer room.** Computers, software, printers, etc. . . . . **$500-$15,000**

## For Those with Disabilities

**Print enlarger** for those unable to read conventional print. . **$3,500**

**Special collection for the disabled,** in the form of Books on Tape, so that visually and physically challenged and learning disabled patrons can use library resources. . . . **$500-$2,000**

## Youth Services

**Puppets for storytime** . . . . . **$50-$75**

**"Ellison" machine** to be used to die cut bookmark shapes . . . . . **$2,500**

**Die sets** for the Ellison machine to cut shapes for bookmarks, etc. . . . . **minimum $500**

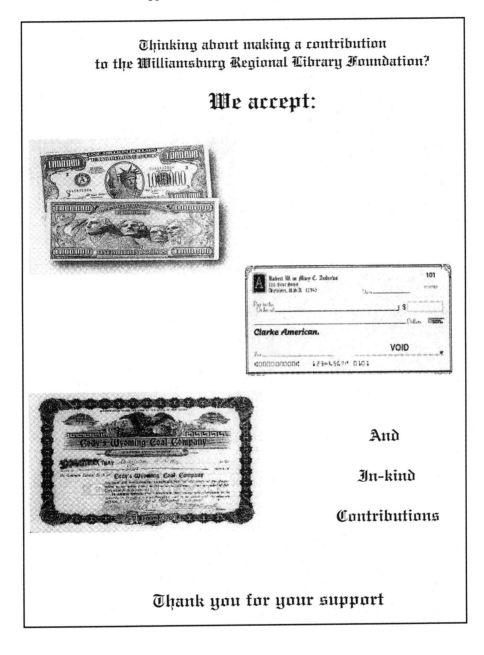

Thinking about making a contribution
to the Williamsburg Regional Library Foundation?

# We accept:

And

In-kind

Contributions

Thank you for your support

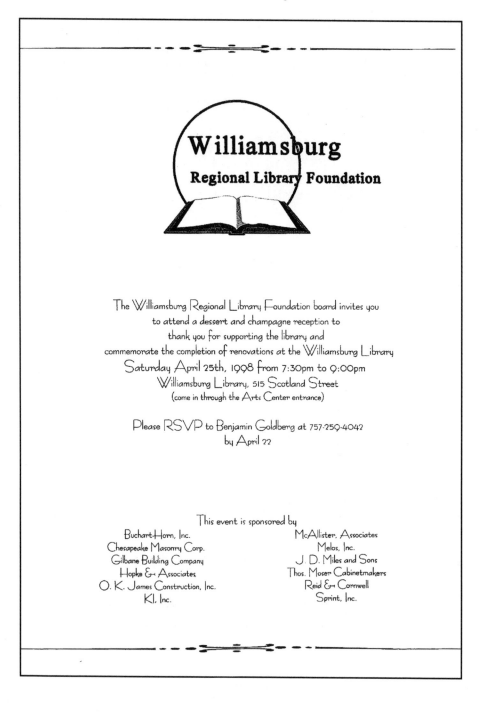

Williamsburg
Regional Library Foundation

The Williamsburg Regional Library Foundation board invites you
to attend a dessert and champagne reception to
thank you for supporting the library and
commemorate the completion of renovations at the Williamsburg Library
Saturday April 25th, 1998 from 7:30pm to 9:00pm
Williamsburg Library, 515 Scotland Street
(come in through the Arts Center entrance)

Please RSVP to Benjamin Goldberg at 757-259-4042
by April 22

This event is sponsored by

Buchart-Horn, Inc.                    McAllister, Associates
Chesapeake Masonry Corp.              Melos, Inc.
Gilbane Building Company              J. D. Miles and Sons
Hopke & Associates                    Thos. Moser Cabinetmakers
O. K. James Construction, Inc.        Reid & Cornwell
KI, Inc.                              Sprint, Inc.

# Thank you to the Sponsors

Buchart-Horn, Inc.

Chesapeake Masonry Corp.

Gilbane Building Company

O. K. James Construction, Inc.

Hopke & Associates

KI, Inc.

McAllister, Associates

Melos, Inc.

J. D. Miles and Sons

Thos. Moser Cabinetmakers

Reid & Cornwell

Sprint, Inc.

# Appendix E:
# It Costs How Much?

The library's two project liaisons were repeatedly surprised at how expensive some building accessories were.

## JCCL

- halogen light bulbs (so beware the architect/designer who really likes these)
- outdoor garbage cans and benches
- meeting room tables

## WL

- marquee at WL
- painted walls in reference area
- cherry wood columns
- precast panels for outside of building

# Appendix F:
# "Best" and "Worst"
# (Staff Comments)

Comments were solicited from staff members on the best and worst results of the construction of JCCL and renovation of WL. Their responses are included here as an example of what can go right and wrong and how some people will see the same result from a different perspective. (Names were changed to protect the innocent and others.)

---

When asked what they thought the best results of construction at JCCL were, staff said:

*Jeanne*
- The solarium reading space and furniture is wonderful.
- The reference workroom space and configuration is even better.
- The many large window walls provide a lot of great light and feeling of openness.
- The kids love the "funny" mirror at the checkout desk.
- The furniture throughout is nice but in the children's area, the tables and chairs, train for returning books, and youth services desk are all especially appropriate.
- The staff lounge area is very nice.

*Gil*
- Spacious quarters in tech services allowing for MUCH-needed personal space (compared to TAFKATS, where discomfort was great and emotions flared).

- Large, windowed cubicle for working.
- Great shelving in my cubicle to store big cataloging books (cataloging tools).
- Desk large enough to accommodate PC, two printers, phone, cataloging tools and have enough space left over to work.
- Large, private staff restroom with "Vacancy" sign in lock.
- Meeting room specifically for staff.
- Tech services dept. head has office with door that can be closed for private consultations, evaluations, meetings, etc.
- Personal, rather than departmental, telephones and voice mail.

*Jack*
- Wide open space.
- Proximity of circ and ref desks to each other and to the public entrance.
- Good use of color and natural/artificial light.
- Shelving (looks good, spaced evenly, not busy).
- Staff goes in one entrance, so there is a spot to always "catch" staff with a note as needed.

*Edward*
- Large open spaces, with lots of natural and artificial light.
- Shelving with backs.
- Nice meeting/conference rooms.
- Nice children's crafts space.
- Lots of parking.
- Nice staff lounge area/away from patron area, but easily accessible.
- Large tech. services area.
- Comfortable work chairs.
- PCs for staff.
- Large mailroom adjacent to delivery door.

*Sandy*
- Children's storage closet.
- Children's signs.
- Shelves.
- Lots of natural light.
- Reading windows.
- Neon sign.
- Spaciousness.
- Flip down shelves in rest rooms.

- Parking.
- Small meeting rooms.

*Ron*
- Plenty of parking.
- Open space inside.
- Natural lighting.
- Adult and youth atriums.
- Community room.
- Staff meeting room.
- Single, welcoming entranceway.

*Chip*
- Colors, design, furniture in children's area.
- Sticking to our guns about color throughout library.
- Having enough space to create adequate workstations for staff and public.
- Lots of parking.
- Great staff chairs for workstations.
- Very workable design for floorboxes (power, cable connections).
- Cable-rich Community Room, equipped for conferences, training sessions.
- Good sized in-floor tracks for cable, making for easy addition of cable.

---

When asked what they thought the worst results of construction at JCCL were, staff said:

*Jeanne*
- The check out waiting area for patrons is right in front of the reference desk.
- The reference shelving is too small an area and puts a lot of limitation on the collection.
- The "wide-open" design and circles of carpet encourage small children to run up and down or jump from one to the other.

*Gil*
- Project was way behind schedule from very early on.
- JCCL did not come through on their commitment to handle purchasing of automated equipment, leaving us to scramble at the last minute to get even the barest necessities to open.

- No storage planned or provided for general library needs.
- Poorly designed children's desk (though eye-catching in appearance).
- A/C system that has had breakdowns and malfunctions from the start.
- No separated space for computer equipment in the projector room.
- Poor landscaping and even worse maintenance.
- Glary lights in staff areas requiring retrofitting in some areas.
- Inadequate cable in graphics room.

### Jack

- Perceived as remote by many patrons.
- Staff office windows look "institutional."

### Edward

- Uncomfortable chairs in workstation.
- Obnoxious, annoying heating/ cooling noises, ALL day long over cubicle.
- Too-cold a/c in summer and fall, too cold in winter and spring.
- No sofa in break room for much-needed, healthy naps.
- Not much "future space" planned (for ex. shelving in Friends mailroom area).
- Not enough general storage space.

### Sandy

- Lighting in some staff areas.
- HVAC system noise.
- Problems getting computers.

### Ron

- Lack of tackable walls where they were supposed to be.
- Carpeting under the neon sign.
- More tile than carpet in the children's program room.
- Children's chairs with holes in the fabric.
- Lack of shelving in the children's workroom.
- Not enough windows that can be opened.
- Tables in library program rooms too heavy for easy set up.
- Lack of phones in the work room.
- Air conditioning problems that persist year after year.
- Summer glare off concrete at staff entrance.

### Chip

- Lack of storage space.

- HVAC noise/other acoustical challenges in the Community Room.
- Expensive, heavy meeting room tables.
- Non-durable chair coverings in children's.

*Bill*

- Some lights are ridiculously expensive to buy due to type of fixture.
- Public bathrooms— needed seamless counters, better quality low flush toilet.
- Staff bathroom — better quality low flush toilet. We didn't want tampon trash container to be inserted in wall, but was done anyway.
- Bigger capacity refrigerator for staff (small freezer area).
- Really needed more and better storage area(s) for facilities equipment and supplies.
- First alarm system was impossible to re-program without bringing in out of town technician (has been replaced by one that's same as WL).
- Children's program room floor hard to keep shiny, tables so heavy, they scrape wax right off.

---

When asked what they thought the best results of construction at WL were, staff said:

*Jeanne*

- Periodical shelving.
- Adult reference area (spacious but cozy).
- Children's desk and ramp.
- Schell Room.
- Children's program room.

*Gil*

- Children's director's office.
- Glass window up the ramp from children's to adult.
- Art display space and tackable walls.
- Color scheme.
- Children's workroom.
- New loading dock.
- Fiber optics over YS program room.
- Computer alcoves.
- Furniture in adult services.
- Children's program room rather than the old amphitheater.

*Jack*

- Reference area, especially the light fixtures.
- More staff room.
- Basement remodel.
- Schell Room.
- Bathrooms remodel.
- Light in children's and reference areas.
- New elevator.
- Ramp redo from adult to YS sections.
- More study/homework areas.
- PCs for staff.

*Edward*

- Thos. Moser furniture in adult services.
- New children's program room.
- Expanded reference shelving.
- Accessible Friends book nook area.
- Staff lounge.
- Automatic doors (at least at one entrance).

*Sandy*

- Project came in on time throughout, thanks to Gilbane.
- Building ambiance.
- Colors, fabrics, wall-coverings throughout building.
- Furniture in adult public area.
- Chandeliers in adult reading areas.
- Fiber optic display in children's area.
- Great landscaping and good upkeep of it.
- Net100 — they did a superb, professional job of cabling.

---

Asked what they thought the worst results at WL were, staff said:

*Jeanne*

- Leaks remain.
- No line of sight between service desks.
- Too many public entrances.

*Gil*

- Children's storage closet that you can't store things in.
- Railings up the ramp.

- Lack of defined teen area.
- Parking.
- Lack of display shelving.
- Phones in workroom.
- Lack of expansion space for books down the road.
- Lack of storage and shelving in children's workroom.
- No storage for program room tables and chairs (can't use the closet designed for them).
- Only one place for a PAC in the non-fiction stacks.

*Jack*

- Still have "closed in" feeling in adult fiction stacks.
- Lighting in much of adult circulating areas seems inadequate.
- Hard to see patrons/ref from Circulation desk.
- The ROOF.

*Edward*

- Climate control between children's/program services and rest of library.
- Resulting public elevator.
- People have trouble finding public service desks.
- Winds around too much — hard to give directions to go from one end of the building to the other.
- Parking across the street.
- Doors open directly in line with circulation desk, making staff and patrons cold during winter months.

*Sandy*

- Cables cut to certain areas of the building without consultation as to the impact nor even information about the reduction, causing library to pay to add this back later in order to provide required services.
- Not enough power outlets to accommodate required automated equipment as well as task lights.
- Poor staff furniture and workstations.
- Poorly designed children's desk.
- Inadequate floor boxes for cable; selected without consideration of functionality.
- Closed in feeling at circulation desk area.
- Repeater room too small.

*Ron*

- The position of the "new and notable" materials.
- The periodical shelving is one tier too high.

*Chip*

- Real office or at least cubby for facilities maintenance staff.
- Adequate storage for facilities supplies and equipment.
- Needed washable paint throughout, corner guards or protective coverings everywhere a cart might bump.
- Install lawn sprinklers during renovation, not after.
- New bathrooms—we didn't want tampon trash receptacles to be inserted in stalls, but they did anyway.
- Bulletin boards—impossible to tack info on them because need long tacks.
- Facilities floor sink near Friends area was removed but never replaced in the mechanical room. The new one up front near circ desk is great, but staff have to slop water over carpet from there to other parts of building.
- Many overlooked items not removed from ceilings, roof, etc. e.g., leaky skylight, open pipes, etc.
- Children's windows not correctly caulked—water rushed in.
- Roof leaks still.

# Bibliography

## *Articles*

Charbeneau, Brett, and Kurzeja, Karen. "Remote but Not Alone: Community Outreach Can Mean Taking the Books to Patrons When They Can't Come to You." *Computers in Libraries*, April 1999, Vol. 19, Number 4. Westport, Connecticut: 20–22, 24–26. (Written by WRL employees about the experiences of setting up and operating the Kids Book Xpress.)

Woodward, Jeannette. "Countdown to a New Library: A Blueprint for Success." *American Libraries: The Magazine of the American Library Association*. April 1999, Vol. 30, Number 4. Chicago: 44–47. (Woodward talks about keeping practicality in mind when choosing furnishings for a new library. This article is adapted from Woodward's book *Countdown to a New Library*.)

## *Books*

Batco, Anthony J., and Richard E. Thompson. "Building a New Library." *Trustee Facts File*. Chicago: Illinois Library Trustees Association, 1986. (Matter of fact, step by step presentation actions to take for library construction. Includes: selecting a library building consultant, selecting an architect, selecting a site, etc. Standard things you should know and do listing of how to build a library genre.)

Brawner, Lee B., and Donald K. Beck, Jr. *Determining Your Public Library's Future Size. A Needs Assessment and Planning Model*. Chicago: American Library Association, 1996. (Relies heavily on input from a library consultant and why a library construction consultant is important. Does not include importance of staff input. Fine primer. Interesting chapter on reading schematics— includes them, then includes criticisms of them. But really just raising placement issues in the blueprint, rather than how to read blueprints.)

Cohen, Aaron, and Elaine Cohen. *Designing and Space Planning for Libraries, A Behavioral Guide*. New York: R. R. Bowker, 1979. (Discusses some psychological issues to consider when constructing and furnishing a library, such as a patron's personal space, wall color, visual responses, etc. Parts are outdated by the fact that libraries today offer a greater variety of resources than in 1979.)

Curzon, Susan C. *Managing Change: A How-To-Do-It Manual for Planning, Implementing, and Evaluating Change in Libraries.* New York: Neal-Schuman, 1989. (Literally a step by step guide for a leader managing change at a public library. Tries to outline managing techniques as well as anticipating responses to change by staff, patrons, etc. to enable the manager to make changes go more smoothly and easily for everyone. Each chapter talks about different changes that need to be managed during a construction project, largely organized by a standard construction timeline. Starts with conceptualizing, then preparing the organization all the way through to evaluating.)

Dahlgren, Anders. *Planning the Small Public Library Building.* Small Libraries Publications, no. 11. Chicago: American Library Association, 1985. (An overview of ALA party line information on library construction. Includes space estimates from 1962 [outdated since they do not take into consideration space for technology services]. Includes a bibliography of other reference sources that may be of interest to those considering a construction project.)

Hagloch, Susan B. *Library Building Projects: Tips for Survival.* Englewood, Colorado: Libraries Unlimited, 1994. (Survival tips, just as the title implies.)

Hall, Richard B. *Financing Public Library Buildings.* New York: Neal-Schuman, 1994. (Discusses funding options, method, and how to best invest funds. The book "was written to provide library managers, trustees, library friends, and government officials with the necessary information to plan and finance a public library construction project.")

Hlavka, Gailyn L., and Thomas J. Madigan. *Planning a Library: A Building Program Model.* Fairfax, Virginia: Fairfax County Public Library, 1983. (Hlavka was building project manager and Madigan was technical consultant on the project. Presented before the construction began. Provides documents related to starting a building program in the form of memoranda and equipment/needs lists.)

Holt, Raymond M. *Wisconsin Library Building Project Handbook.* Madison: Wisconsin Department of Public Instruction, 1990. (Contains good information about the process from beginning to end. Written to help libraries prepare and plan for library construction. Addresses all the standard aspects of a construction project, such as overview, needs assessment, accessibility issues, furniture space, etc. Only problem is under role of the librarian, library consultant and architect, librarian is only a page, library consultant is just over a page and architect is about four pages. Written by a library consultant, so it's from his perspective. Includes in appendix an example letter of inquiry to an architect.)

Karp, Rashelle S. (ed.). *Part-Time Public Relations with Full-Time Results: A PR Primer for Libraries.* Chicago: American Library Association, 1995. (Provides tips for public relations that can be used during a construction project.)

Martin, Ron G. (ed.). *Libraries for the Future: Planning Buildings That Work. Papers from the LAMA Library Buildings Preconference June 27–28, 1991.* Chicago: American Library Association, 1992. (A compilation of essays that review different aspects of building projects. One essay is by Anders Dahlgren [authored *Planning the Small Public Library*]. Subtitle to his essay is "An Overly Simplified Summary of What Will Be Visited upon You When you Build a Building." Good outline of the process involved, good starting point. Reviews trends, issues, planning teams, players, selecting architects, etc.)

McBomb, Dana Quick. *Public Library Buildings: Their Financing, Design, Construction, Equipment and Operation*. Los Angeles: Los Angeles Public Library, 1935. (Of interest for two reasons. Interesting from a historical perspective — more than 60 years ago many of the questions and answers being asked about library construction were the same as today. During five years as superintendent of buildings at the L.A. Public Library, the author was a part of the construction of many libraries in the area — as he points out himself, his experiences "cannot but be of very material value to many others...." Dated to be sure, but certain truths persevere. [Ex.: In all cases, the ideas of the board and librarians should be written out in detail, so there may be no possible misunderstanding on the part of the architect concerning the ideas and desires of these authorities.])

Oehlerts, Donald E. *Books and Blueprints; Building America's Public Libraries*. New York: Greenwood Press, 1991. (Academic study of the 120 largest and most costly libraries built between 1850 and 1989. Examines changing ideas about architecture and library service as reflected in the planing and construction of the buildings.)

Sannwald, William. W. *Checklist of Library Building Design Considerations*, 3rd edition. Chicago: American Library Association, 1997. (Detailed checklist of questions that should be asked by libraries before and during construction or renovation. Does not include any discussion on analyzing the results of filling out any given checklist.)

Smith, Lester K. (ed.). *Planning Library Buildings: From Decision to Design. Papers from a Library Administration and Management Association Buildings and Equipment Section Preconference at the 1984 American Library Associations Annual Conference, Dallas, Texas*. Chicago: American Library Association, 1986. (A compilation of essays that review different aspects of building projects. It includes discussions on needs assessments, planning teams, evaluations schematics, and climate control. Chapter 11 does admit that architects speak and write a different language that must be learned. Attempts to teach how to read blueprints, by example [one gets to flip back and forth between author's written example and the blueprints].)

Stephenson, Mary Sue. *Planning Library Facilities: A Selected, Annotated Bibliography*. Metuchen, New Jersey: Scarecrow, 1990. (Eight hundred sources on library construction published from 1970 to 1988. Divided into categories, Facility, Planning, Design, Evaluation and Renovation; Housing and Serving the User, Staff and Collection; Environmental, Mechanical, Electrical, and Security Systems. Each section has subcategories.)

Watkins, Jan. *Programming Author Visits*. Chicago: American Library Association, 1996. (Provides tips for public relations that can be used during a construction project.)

# About the Contributors

**Sherle Elizabeth Abramson** is currently electronic reference services coordinator with the Library of Virginia. She earned her bachelor of arts in English with a minor in philosophy at the University of Virginia and her master's of library science at University of Maryland. During construction of JCCL, Abramson helped plan the public computer room, set up the public Internet stations, design the modular arrangement for the reference workroom and defeat the Monolith.

**Noreen Bernstein,** youth services director, WRL for 13 years. She earned her AB from Barnard College and her master's of library science from University of Maryland. She was responsible for the design of youth services during construction and selected the original illustration for both buildings.

**Margaret (Peg) Bradshaw** has been the collection services director at Williamsburg Regional Library since 1994. In 1999 she received an award for outstanding service from James City County, Virginia. Bradshaw served as the library's project liaison during the renovation and expansion of the Williamsburg Library.

**Brett Charbeneau** is the library's network administrator and is charged with keeping computer technology functional and up to date. Charbeneau did his undergraduate work at the College of William and Mary and has received fellowships from Brown University, the Virginia Historical Society, and the American Antiquarian Society for his work with descriptive bibliography. Besides keeping the library's network relatively secure, Charbeneau is also involved with keeping the bookmobile connected to the network using wireless technology.

**Gregory Dunkle** is a project manager for Gilbane Building Company in their South Eastern District Office. He has project responsibilities for a $57 million luxury high-rise in Atlanta, Georgia. Dunkle served as project manager on the Williamsburg Library project and was responsible for all projects managed by Gilbane for the City of Williamsburg, including the Matthew Whaley renovation, water treatment plant and the Williamsburg parking garage and park renovation.

**Andrew Faber** is the regional operations manager for Gilbane Building Company in their Mid-Atlantic Regional Office. He has operations responsibility for Gilbane projects in the Mid-Atlantic states. Faber served as project executive on the Williamsburg Library project and was responsible for all services provided by Gilbane to the City of Williamsburg.

**Bernard Farmer, Jr.,** is a licensed engineer employed by James City County, Virginia. Farmer has nearly 25 years professional experience in the construction industry with the U. S. Army, as a designer and project manager in the library industry, as a local government code official, and most recently as a manager of various construction projects.

**Shirley Floyd** is the education liaison reference librarian at WRL. She works on the reference desk at both locations and is responsible for outreach to assisted living centers for seniors in the form of book talks. In addition, she provides liaison with middle and high school teachers and media specialists. Floyd earned her degree from the University of Illinois.

**Judith Fuss** is systems administrator with the Williamsburg Regional Library, overseeing the operation of the automated library system. She began her work in libraries behind the circulation desk, developing programs for training circulation staff. She received a bachelor of science in social welfare from Pennsylvania State University and was a contributor to "Managing Overdues: A How-To-Do-It Manual for Libraries."

**Benjamin J. Goldberg** received his bachelor of arts from Bard College and master's and doctoral degrees from the College of William and Mary. He is the director of development and volunteer coordinator at the Williamsburg Regional Library. Goldberg came to the library during the first phase of the Williamsburg Library renovation. He served as first editor for this book.

**Patrick S. Golden** has been program services director for the Williamsburg Regional Library system since May 1995. The program services department he manages is responsible for the development and promotion of adult library programs as well as public meeting room support for the library system. He holds a master of arts in education degree from the College of William and Mary and is the co-author of "The Educator's Guide to the Internet" (Addison-Wesley Publishing Co., 1997).

**Betty Guernsey** worked at WRL for seven years in technical services and 13 in reference. She earned her master's of library science from UC Berkeley. During construction Guernsey worked on the reference desk and was one of the people who helped clear out the desk in an hour, when the construction company claimed that space without notice.

**Patsy J. Hansel**, now director of the Mesa (Arizona) Public Library, was WRL's director during the construction periods covered by our book. She has an undergraduate degree from the University of North Carolina at Charlotte, a master's in history from Wake Forest University and a master's of science in library science from the University of North Carolina at Chapel Hill. She is now working on construction projects with the staff of the Mesa Public Library. She served as an editor for this book.

**Jean Kelly** has been a reference librarian in adult services at WRL for over 12 years. During construction of the JCCL and renovation of the WL, she planned and reorganized all interlibrary loan operations from a one-building operation to a system-wide one without interruption of service. She, along with the other reference librarians, made opening day book selections, especially for the adult fiction collection of the JCCL.

**Jeanette Navia** is the adult non-fiction and authority control cataloger at WRL. During the construction of JCCL, she helped specify the cataloging and processing needs for the book and audio-visual materials.

**Genevieve Owens** is support services director, managing automated, delivery, and technical services. She spent ten years in academic libraries before coming to WRL, and she is active in the collection management and development section of ALA's Association for Library Collections and Technical Services. She assumed responsibility for a number of remaining construction issues at the JCCL just as it was set to go out of warranty, and she assisted with telephone planning and installation at the WL.

**Elizabeth C. Parker** is WRL's human resources and facilities director. Parker is a graduate of UCLA with a degree in pictorial arts and served as a public health nurse, midwife, and English and art teacher with the Peace Corps in Brazil. She worked extensively in various publishing ventures before joining the WRL team in 1978.

**Vanessa Patrick** is an architectural historian, whose brief but happy career as a reference librarian began with the opening of JCCL and concluded with the implementation of the WRL genealogy center, the Family History Station. She holds master's degrees in architectural history and library science.

**Jennifer Payne** is the graphics artist at WRL. During the renovation of WL, Payne created most of the signs, flyers, and pamphlets that informed the public about the project. She earned her degree from Virginia Tech.

**Cecilia Schmidt** is acquisitions manager and handles the vendor transactions for the library collection materials purchases. She has worked on almost all of the library committees at one time or another. Schmidt supervised the ordering, receipt, and payment for all of the direct order materials for the opening day collection and authorized payment of all materials invoices received from the main opening day vendor.

**Kirstin Steele** has been the assistant director at Williamsburg Regional Library since 1996. She graduated from the College of William and Mary and received her master's of library science from the University of Alabama at Tuscaloosa. She serves on the Intellectual Freedom Committee of the Virginia Library Association and on the Public Library Data Service Publication Committee of the Public Library Association. Steele was the library's liaison for the James City County Library construction project. She served as an editor for this book.

**Caryn Strauss-Smith** holds a bachelor of science from Johns Hopkins University. She has worked at WRL since 1993. As someone on the circulation desk, she handled many patron questions and complaints about the construction work at WL.

# Index